the intelligent guide to your financial future

the intelligent guide to your financial future

intelligent investing

intelligent retirement planning

intelligent estate planning and asset protection

By: Norbert Mindel, PFS, JD, CPA, CFP®
      Marcus Heinrich, CFP®
      David Strulowitz, JD, LLM
      With Steve Percifield, ASB

Contents

This book is dedicated to our families, friends, and clients

Norbert Mindel
Marcus Heinrich
David Strulowitz

Foreword

This is not a get-rich-quick book on how to make millions in real estate and stocks; rather, our message is for individuals who have accumulated some wealth and are looking for an intelligent, long-term financial strategy that they can live with. We assume that you—like hundreds of millions of others—have probably learned that in the vast, vast majority of cases, the wisdom of Wall Street simply doesn't work.

The material described in this book comes largely from academic research that has been subject to peer review. This is important because academics are not *paid* to develop a product to sell you. They can, therefore, retain their objectivity.

The authors of this book have each spent over twenty years in the financial planning and investment industry. They have seen every pitch spin and investment mutation one can think of and, sadly, have come away with the conclusion that not only is it not *pretty* out there, but it is *dangerous* for individual investors.

Intelligent financial planning has several interpretations based on the context it is used. For example, it means having wills, trusts, and durable powers to ensure your wishes are taken care of when you are incapacitated or at your death. It also means protecting your net worth in the event of catastrophic health by having long-term care insurance. It also means protecting yourself from liability by having an umbrella liability-insurance policy, but in the context of investments, it means having a "sustainable strategy." As will be illustrated throughout the first three chapters of this book, there may be other intelligent strategies at any point in time, but very few can be sustained due either to your risk tolerance or the inherent risk of the strategy. Accordingly, when we use the term "sustainable," think intelligent. After all, what is the point of having the smartest strategy that lasts for only one year or several years when your goals are for a lifetime?

Every day, Wall Street must create products to sell you in order to make a profit. They then must convince their sales forces they *are* great products. The sales force, in turn, must convince you to *buy* the product in order for them to earn a commission. Even giving Wall Street the benefit of the doubt, this does not seem to be a process that has *your* best interest at heart.

Every day, you are told about every conceivable type of investment, what is in and what is out. The cable channels bring out their experts who tell you what to buy and what to sell. And, every day, the advice is different. Have you ever thought *if they are so smart, why do they have to work every day to convince me to buy their investment product? Why don't they live off their own investment product?*

We live in an age of unprecedented access to information. Yet when we use this information to buy "great stocks" of "great companies," it seems we lose money. Our observation is that, many times, an individual's emotions—excitement over a purported opportunity for example—is more important than the actual investment. This can be the most destructive factor in growing your portfolio.

In chapter 3, we describe the results of a study done by DALBAR, which show that although the equity market in a twenty-year period ending in 2003 grew 12.35 percent the average equity investor earned only 2.67 percent. Why? Is it listening to all those smart people on TV, or the magazine you bought for $3 that told you this month's hot stocks and mutual funds, or your stockbroker calling you to tell you today's hot tip?

The bottom line is equities (that is, stocks where you own a piece of the company) will probably outperform most other asset classes (such as bonds) over the long run.

However, the long run *can* be a problem. It *is* a problem for Wall Street, since they need you to buy and sell *today*, and it *is* a problem for most individual investors who—twenty years ago—held funds for twelve years or longer and now hold them for less than two years.

To have a chance of succeeding with your personal investment strategy, you need to eliminate the Wall Street mentality of buying what is hot (and selling what is not). You also need to control your emotions and biases. To do this requires two things:

1. *A sustainable strategy*—you need a long-term strategy in order to achieve long-term gains. This requires gathering assets that you can live with rather than jumping from investment to investment trying to pick winners.
2. *An independent advisor*—that is primarily compensated on a fee basis, who earns your trust by helping you develop your investment strategy and keeps your emotions in check.

Our goals in writing this book are to

1. Eliminate misconceptions that cost investors' money, even as they line the pockets of Wall Street firms
2. Provide you with a new investment philosophy that will allow you to successfully plan your investment success
3. Show you how to plan and protect your retirement
4. Help you preserve your estate for your descendants

We urge you to read this book through and incorporate what you will learn into your own investment, retirement, and estate-planning strategies. We also urge you to seek out the advice of professionals in this regard as a career of experience in these specialized subjects is an essential requirement for helping you implement many of these strategies.

Acknowledgements

If you noticed the alphabet soup following the names of the authors on the cover, it is a result of the fact that all of them are highly qualified, certified experts in their fields, with proven histories of success in their endeavors.

If you observed my name on the cover, you may have observed my affiliation credentials: ASB. It's there because I was jealous. If you have familiarity with the fields of law, finance, or accounting, you recognized accreditation of the authors. ASB, however, probably leaves you scratching your head. Well, it stands for American Society of Baking.

I've been involved in the bakery industry all my life, spending most of my career in bakery marketing, writing, and publishing. So naturally, when the authors needed someone to put a book together for them, they came to me. Why, because I knew absolutely nothing about the subject matter.

The ignorance I brought to this project was invaluable because if I could understand what they were trying to convey, anyone could!

In addition (and on a more serious note), besides the authors themselves, special thanks and appreciation is due the following:

Susan Reedy Williams, JD, for her expertise and contributions in the estate-planning area.
Shannon Dawson, CPA, CFA, for her insightful comments on our subject matter, and diligent review of our initial manuscript.
Michelle Barbiere, Laura Gornto, and Patty Ahern, for their tremendous help with our graphic material.
Debra Carpenter CLU, CHFC, for her expertise and contributions regarding long-term health care.
Debbie Manno and Allison Tronnes, Marcus and Norm's assistants, for making us better financial advisors.
Richard T. Reibman, JD, who not only contributed the section on "Understanding Basic Asset Protection Principles," but may be the only

attorney in the world to have ever done something of this nature for free, as he allowed himself to be badgered into it by Norbert, and it only cost him an iPod.

We also want to thank the following advisors for their expertise, insight, and significant contributions that made this book possible: **John Adam, EA, CFP®; Joseph Spokas, CPA, CFP®; Mark Finke, CFP®; Charles Surdyke, CFP®; Thomas Mengel, CLU, CHFC, MSFS; Thomas Murphy; and Alan Hambourger, CPA,CFP®, PFS.**

Steve Percifield, March 29, 2005

Introduction

We use the word "intelligent" on the cover of the book repeatedly. Not only because no one would read a book about unintelligent investing, but also because intelligent starts with the letter "I."

While this book does demystify intelligent investment, provides for intelligent planning of your retirement, and provides basic guidelines for intelligent planning of your estate, there is another reason the "I" is so prominent on our cover. Because, it can be used as the personal pronoun you would use to refer to yourself. From your standpoint, this book is about strategies that will help you achieve the financial future that you desire. It will help you answer the following question. "How can *I* get the most out of my investments, retire comfortably, and leave the most to my heirs?"

You already have some wealth and have intelligently managed to keep much of what you've accumulated. Perhaps you have built a successful business, or worked hard over many years steadily putting money away, or perhaps you have unfortunately lost a spouse or beloved family member to whom you were devoted. Regardless of how you came by your wealth, a primary tenant of this book is that your financial decisions from now on should most benefit *you* and not *Wall Street*.

It was only a few years ago when we were all going to be wealthy!

The stock market was growing at 30 percent per annum. Everyone made money in the markets, confirming to them that they were all financial geniuses. Millions upon millions of people, who had never invested before, jumped into the market with both feet—especially into the high-tech sector—in order to ride the apparent *momentum*. And because of their initial successes, they stayed as even more new investors came in.

With an increasing corps of buyers, very reluctant sellers, and with additional stock purchases being sought faster than new issues could be created, prices of even dog-ugly stocks soared due to simple supply and demand, with little attention paid to their underlying values.

Investors of all persuasions patted themselves on their backs for having the "wisdom" to invest and earn such high returns. They continued to pour even more money into the market, sustaining the market's upward momentum.

Physicists tell us that *momentum* is the tendency of an object in motion to stay in motion or an object at rest to stay at rest . . . until acted upon by some outside force. So it is with the market—an entity so complex—that the numbers of forces acting upon it are all but infinite. But those myriad forces *did*, in fact, act upon the upward momentum of the market, bringing it first to an abrupt stop, and then a reversal. And the rest, as they say, is history.

During the '90s, a lot of investors showed a lot of gains—before the bottom fell out. Then they lost a lot of those gains—in some cases, all of them and more. But guess what (and this is the reason this book was written); they didn't *have* to suffer such losses. And if they had been heeding common sense and proven, award-winning financial theory (rather than the conventional wisdom of Wall Street), they wouldn't have.

There are five underlying premises to this book:

- Market forces are far too complex to be either fully understood, predictable, *or exploited* by *anyone* (including Wall Street or media "experts," or—for that matter—yourself).
- Anyone *can*, however, reduce the market losses produced by normally recurring market "adjustments," by using modern, proven theories of portfolio management that are explained herein.
- By incorporating the above into a strategy of passive management using a fee-based professional advisor rather than a commission-based Wall Street agent (discussed later), you can turn your investment and retirement futures into achievable plans rather than a crapshoot.
- The key to creating wealth in a portfolio is not having the best strategy at any point in time but having a sustainable strategy over the long term.
- Once you have created wealth, you need to protect it.

We intend to convince you, the reader, that there is no guru out there that has the answer on how to beat the market. Putting aside the likes of Warren Buffet, one of the few who has arguably done just that, most investors are destined for below-average returns as they attempt to beat the market! Think of the irony; investors spurn mediocrity because average is not good enough, and as a result, their return is below average.

If you are a little skeptical, we understand; after all, you probably know someone who always makes a killing in the market. Right, just like the people you know who go to Las Vegas, who always win and never lose.

The fact you have read this far suggests that you believe in the principles of free-market capitalism; you are financially successful in your chosen field; and success has provided you with investment capital for which you wish to obtain the greatest possible return with the least amount of risk

If the above describes you and your situation, what follows is probably going to change everything you've thought or been told regarding your investment strategy. It details:

- The history of failure resulting from trying to ride market momentum
- Why Wall Street may be your enemy in planning your investments
- Why the financial press might be your *worst* source of investment information
- How to understand and use modern portfolio theory
- Why high risk does *not* necessarily equate with high reward
- How diversification can provide you with greater average returns *and* greater safety at the same time
- How to develop a sustainable strategy that will last your lifetime
- How your assets can be converted to meet the income needs of your golden years
- How your assets can best be protected
- How your estate can provide the most to those you leave behind
- Why fee-based professional advice is needed to meet your goals

To make what is an admittedly dry topic more relevant to our readers' real-life situations; we start out with financial "myths," which we then proceed to explode with the light of reality. These, in turn, are followed by what should and shouldn't be done to ensure your long-term success.

We sincerely hope you will read this short book to its conclusion and incorporate its recommendations into your own financial planning, for your benefit and that of your family.

Section I

Growing Your Long Term Wealth by Changing Your Investment Philosophy

Chapter I

Financial Pornography

or

Fear and Loathing on Wall Street

The Myth of the Altruistic Wall Street Investment Professional

A regional vice president of a world-renowned institutional investment firm took a prime potential client to a yacht harbor in Boca Rotan, to wine, dine, and impress him.

"There," he said pointing to a 120-footer moored in the harbor, "is our president's yacht. "And there," he said, pointing at a sixty-foot sport fisherman across the inlet "is our executive vice president's fishing boat. "And here," he said smugly, stepping out onto the gangway aside a 52-foot cockpit motor yacht, "is my baby."

"Sweet," the client replied, feigning admiration. "I have only one question: Where are your clients' boats?"

Although not mythical, there's an old down-home saying built upon grass-roots wisdom that should be kept in mind as you read this section:

"Even a blind squirrel finds a nut once in a great while."

Most of Wall Street's investors' victories are built upon this sort of luck.

The charlatans of ancient times earned their keeps by making predictions which, even though largely inaccurate, were popular with the well-placed individuals who paid for them. The viability of their predictions, then as today, was "proven" by citing the occasional exception in which they were correct.

The services of the charlatans were popular because the wealthy *wanted* to believe that their positions, connections, and ability to *pay* for the charlatans' services gave them a divine insight into the future.

In today's high-tech, secular, and democratic society, the role of the charlatan has shifted away from predictions regarding fate, God, and nature. And the advice of today's charlatans, thanks to the democratizing influence of cheaply accessible mass media, is more readily available to a much larger audience.

Today's charlatans predict the future of the markets and substantiate their credibility by citing the relatively few instances in which they are correct. The audience gladly accepts the charlatans' advice as it promises to reward them with increased wealth and power.

But as you read on, remember these two things:

- No one has the ability to predict the long-term activity of the market.
- It is proven (as you shall see) that your investment strategy *has* to be built upon longer term considerations, as opposed to making occasional *right guesses* on short-term investments.

Understanding What You Can't Understand

Please reread the heading of this section. It's a bit of a paradox. Our purpose here is not to explain the mysteries of a market that you don't—currently—understand, far from it in fact. Our purpose here is to explain to you how much you don't understand. And why—for that matter—neither you, nor we, nor the most renowned experts in the world ever *will*. There is simply too much information and too many variables for *anyone* to accurately predict market behavior.

As counterintuitive as it may seem, knowing how much you don't (and can't) know about the behavior of financial markets is the first step toward ensuring your long-term success in them.

So let's explode a few myths, right off the bat.

The myth: *Concentrate your investments in those stocks you "know" are going to be winners.*

The reality: *The dynamics of the economy are too unpredictable to take such a potentially catastrophic risk.*

The collective "smarts" of every financial advisor, every fund manager, every economist, and every politician in the world, compared to the dynamics driving the economy, are like a fly on an elephant's back.

Just as the fly is unable to either predict or influence the direction in which the elephant is going to travel, so is it impossible for any individual or group to control or predict the future movements of a free market. Even a controlled market must eventually relinquish itself to the greater influence of market dynamics, hence, the demise of Communism, and the long-term, continuing growth of free-market economies.

The Parallels Between Planned Economies and Actively Managed Portfolios

In an opening statement in debate with Donald Yachtman at the Schwab Institutional conference in San Francisco in October of 1995, Rex Sinquefield observed that economic theory, empirical research, and history all supported the concept that a free-market economy was efficient. He also observed that a managed economy was inherently doomed to mediocrity or failure. He, for many of the same reasons, drew parallels between a managed economy and a "managed" stock portfolio.

Sinquefield alluded to the twentieth century's flirtations with planned economies under Socialism and Communism, noting that (at the time of his comments) only two rigidly controlled economies remained in the world—North Korea and Cuba (neither one exactly an economic powerhouse). Those economies which have continued to grow have flourished under either relatively free markets or markets in which economic freedoms have been greatly expanded (such as mainland China's).

In comparing the similarities of managed economies with managed portfolios, Sinquefield observed that "it is my contention that active management does not make sense theoretically and isn't justified empirically." Sinquefield implied that management of entire economies or of individual stock portfolios, in order to obtain optimal results, is impossible due to the shear complexity of the underlying dynamics.

Free markets, on the other hand, rely upon the collective wisdom of billions of individual purchase decisions to direct them.

"So who still believes markets don't work?" Sinquefield asked rhetorically. "Apparently it is only North Koreans, the Cubans and . . . *active managers.*"

Active managers would include the Wall Street professionals who actively trade equities and securities in an effort to *control* the returns of the portfolios from which they were derived. He continued that "it's easy to understand the allure, the seductive power, of active management. After all, it's exciting fun to dip and dart, pick stocks and time markets, to get high fees for this, and to do it all with someone *else's* money."

Sinquefield states succinctly what modern portfolio theory suggests and what is proven by empirical market study: the dynamics of the market are so vast as to be incomprehensible to individuals and, therefore, unmanageable by them.

Overall, active management of one's investment portfolio is almost assuredly doomed to failure (as will be demonstrated). But if active management of your portfolio *is* doomed, what actions *can* you take to achieve planned growth of your investments? *Diversification* of one's portfolio, as we will discuss in later chapters, is the answer. It provides a proven means of hedging your investments to offer protection from the erratic gyrations of the market.

Ideal diversification would provide one with investments that were opposites in terms of their reactions to market forces. In this way, the negative impact of conditions on one investment would have a corresponding positive impact on the other, making one immune to wild gyrations in one's total worth, while both investments—over the long term—continued to increase in value. So why not simply put your money into complementary mutual funds?

Investing in well-managed mutual funds, it would seem, is a viable means toward needed diversification. After all, a mutual fund offers not only needed diversification, but a veritable brain trust of professionals, handling those diverse investments for you. But such a strategy is far from foolproof, even if the best funds are selected.

The myth: *Managed mutual funds are an effective way to diversify, offering you safety by spreading out your investments and a good return by placing them in the hands of professional managers.*

The reality: *Fees notwithstanding, actively managed mutual funds have—on average— underperformed when compared to the market as a whole.*

Let's start with the difference between an actively managed mutual fund and a passive fund. With an actively managed fund, the fund manager is basically gambling with your money, betting that he or she can *pick* winning stock trends (later on we demonstrate the futility of these efforts). The work of the manager revolves around actively *buying and selling stocks* on a continuous basis. In a passive fund, however, the work of the fund managers is done up front, ensuring that the *allocation* of the investments will yield the best long-term performance.

If ever there was a time for actively managed fund managers to strut their stuff, the decade of the '90s was it. Even the least sophisticated investors—on average— were racking up significant returns with their stock selections during this boom. And yet, as reported by the *Wall Street Journal* on August 5, 2004, investors would have been better served if fund managers had failed to show up for work.

The journal cited a study by Morningstar, Inc. showing that shareholders in six of ten multibillion-dollar mutual funds that were studied would have earned more over a 4.5-year period, if the fund manager had not traded or repositioned during that time.

Typically, these managers have more market information available to them, and more investing experience, than almost anyone and are experts in their chosen fields. And yet, the majority of the high-profile funds studied not only *underperformed* the market itself, but their clients would have done better if the funds hadn't been managed *at all.*

This, of course, raises a question: If the major fund managers, with all of their sophisticated information networks and analytical capabilities were incapable of picking winners, what chance does a private investor—with his or her limited resources—have? Further, what sources of information *can* be reliably employed to achieve the types of yields you desire?

The myth: *Gathering knowledge is the key to making the right investment decisions. Studying the markets will allow you to pick winners.*
The reality: *A little knowledge is a dangerous thing. A lot of knowledge is even more dangerous. Knowledge cannot predict the future.*

Virtually everyone makes a common mistake when considering their investment decisions; they assume that knowledge is power. Investors further assume that the more knowledge they have, the better their shots at selecting the best investments.

But as already noted, the dynamics of the market are infinitely more complex than the collective genius of the greatest economic and financial minds in the world.

If such is the case, of what benefit is the accumulation of additional knowledge? No matter how much is accumulated, it will still be woefully inadequate. Nevertheless, human nature dictates that investors continue to try to gather as much information as possible in an effort to allow them to make the best financial choices. A lot of this information comes from the print media.

The Failings of the Financial press

There is a downside to freedom of the press: The same freedom that allows someone with something *"worthwhile to say"* to print it, also allows someone with *"nothing to say"* to print it too and pass it off as some kind of informed revelation. With people under pressure from deadlines in periodical publishing, this happens more often than one would want to assume. Worse yet, freedom of the press opens the door to those who have their own agendas, to disseminate the information needed to support them, with only casual concern for the accuracy of such information.

The myth: *"Financial pornography" doesn't really hurt anyone.*
The reality: *"Financial pornography" can destroy portfolios and lives by dealing with investment complexities, far too simply.*

Let's start off with what we mean by "financial pornography."

Funk & Wagnalls defines "pornography" as "obscene literature or art." It further defines "obscene" as "offensive or abhorrent to prevailing concepts of morality or decency." The Supreme Court, using different criteria, defines pornography as something "appealing to prurient interest . . . having no redeeming social value."

By either definition, both the business press and the regular news media could qualify as financial pornographers. They qualify as such by spreading half truths and lies that simplify a highly complex subject (the investment markets) while passing that knowledge off as some kind of divine revelation. Their purpose in doing so, it would appear, is to titillate the *investment voyeurs* in their audience, who imagine they are players in the action. Such titillation increases subscription and newsstand sales revenues for the publications, even as its oversimplification threatens the value of others' investments.

Substitute money for sex (easily done in this day and age, when you stop to dwell on it) and the financial titillation of the investment voyeurs meets both the courts' *and Funk & Wagnall's* definitions of pornography: It flies in the face of currently prevailing morality while offering no redeeming value.

An example:

In the July 26, 2004, issue of *Investment News,* the weekly newspaper for financial advisers, Mike Clowes, editorial director, bemoaned the tough time that financial planners and investment advisers have, trying "to counteract poor advice in the daily newspapers."

Clowes went on to cite a column in a nationally distributed newspaper in which readers were advised to (1) "target winning sectors" (brilliant), (2) *time* the market (who'd have thunk it), and (3) *concentrate* the portfolio (hold on to that one, Gertrude).

Now here (number 3) is a real eyebrow raiser. Putting aside modern portfolio theory and the writing of Nobel Prize-winning economists such as Harry Markowitz, here is a column, in a major newspaper, telling investors that instead of *diversifying* (as a means of hedging against losses), they should *concentrate* their investments and just pick *winners.*

Brilliant! Want assured success for your investments? Then target winning sectors; time your sales to coincide with the peaks and your purchases with the valleys, and limit your purchases to those whose values are sure to increase tremendously.

Well, duh! Thank you so very much. It reminds one of the old skit on *Saturday Night Live* in which an author is being interviewed regarding his book, *How to Make a Million Dollars Without Paying Any Taxes.* When asked to synopsize the advice given in the book, the author says, "It's easy. First, you make a million dollars. Then . . ."

Let's explode a few myths regarding the value of the advice proffered by the business and financial media.

The myth: *The advice of the business experts in the media will help you to pick the right investments at the right times.*
The reality: *The ability of the business press to select winners does not stand up to scrutiny.*

It is almost a given that any informed investor reads business and investment media in order to remain informed. And it is certain that these readings influence their thought processes and decision-making. But it's interesting to note that even these repositories of investor knowledge and informed opinion are less than stellar in their market-prediction accomplishments.

Their writings may not be pornographic by our definitions, but they certainly appear to be flirting with titillation, at least.

Let's look at some of the advice and comments of the financial press and see what pearls of wisdom they have provided in the past to help you, the investor, navigate the complexities of investing. The following are just some examples.

March 3, 1997, *Fortune Magazine.* "America's most admired companies . . . masters of innovation . . . Coca-Cola."

The (actual) return for Coca-Cola, one of the most admired companies in 1997, from March 1, 1997, to December 31, 2002, was -22.74 percent (*minus* nearly 23 percent). *Source: Bloomberg*

February 1998, *Smart Money.* "The Best Mutual Funds for 1998, Fidelity Select Developing Communications, T. Rowe Price Science and Technology"

These funds were top picks. Their one-year returns for 2002 were -47.78 percent and -40.57 percent respectively, and five-year annualized returns ending December 31, 2002, were -2.61 percent and -8.03 percent, respectively. *Source: Lipper*

August 23, 1998, *Forbes.* "Janus, how it became the hot fund family . . . Results put this fund family in a class by itself."

Annualized return for the three largest Janus equity funds August 1, 1999, to December 31, 2002, are shown on the following chart:

Fund	Annualized Return %
Janus Fund	-14.89
Janus Worldwide	-10.16
Janus Twenty	-16.99

Source: Lipper

May 1999, *Money Magazine.* "Everyone's getting rich . . . Here's how to get your share . . . Tech stocks for the next decade."

Of the ten stocks selected, only two experienced a positive price change. The average return was -26.50 percent. *Source: Money Magazine, May 1999; article used March 24, 1999, prices; Morningstar.com (adjusted for stock splits).*

February 2000, *Worth Magazine*. "Asset allocation and diversification can jeopardize an entire investment program. Funds with growth orientation should dominate your portfolio." Robert Markman, Markman Multifunds

Annualized return February 1, 2000, to October 31, 2002:

Fund	Annualized Return %
Markman Aggressive Allocation	-33.72
Markman Moderate Allocation	-25.7
Markman Conservative Allocation	-15.7
S&P 500 Index	-14.06
S&P 500 Growth Index	-18.6

Source: Micropal and *Standard and Poor's*

And so on, and so on, and so on. All in all, it's pretty grim.

The press makes it its business to be the best informed source of financial and investment information available. Yet, with all their sources and resources, their record—based on the above examples (and thousands more not shown)—has been dismal.

Think about it; had you heeded advice, such as that listed above, at the time it was offered, how much money would *you* have lost?

Another investment myth popularized during the go-go '90s that continued even after the market waned revolved around the concept of jumping on to initial public offerings (IPOs) of stocks while they were *still a bargain.*

The myth: *Getting to the top is best accomplished by getting in at the bottom—IPOs are a key to a winning investment strategy.*
The Reality: *Your chances of making it big with an IPO are probably not nearly as good as a trip to Vegas. Do you want to risk it?*

During the '90s, the demand for stocks was so great, and the number of new investors seeking to *enter* the market accelerated so rapidly that new stock issues could not be created quickly enough—a classic case of demand exceeding the available supply.

Voila! Initial public offerings took off like rockets during this time, as demand for a finite number of stock issues drove prices ever upward . . . or did they?

Even during decades of more typical market activity, investors tend to swoon over the relatively few IPOs that "catch fire," without regard for all the ones that flop. Worse yet, they tend to recall the early days, during which the stock was "on fire" without regard to the type of return provided over longer terms. It's the *Las Vegas* mentality: Think of all the times a friend or associate has told you about hitting it big on the roulette wheel or the blackjack table. Those episodes stand out in their minds (and their conversations) to the exclusion of nearly all else.

Now, think about the times a friend or associate bragged about how they earned a much greater return by *not* going to Vegas, staying home, and leaving their gambling money in passbook savings, instead. Even though we know that such is much more likely to be the case, you can't think of anyone who *ever* bragged about it, can you? Everyone remembers (and talks about) their one *winning* stint at the table but conveniently forgets or fails to mention their (many more) *losing* experiences.

So it is with IPOs.

Between 1994 and 1999, of a group of more than ten thousand publicly traded companies, only twenty-nine of them could claim earnings growth of 20 percent each year, according to the economic research department of ThinkEquity. Twenty-nine out of ten thousand—about one-third of 1 percent!

What do you suppose *your* odds would have been of picking the one-third of 1 percent of IPOs that offered you the returns you expected?

According to Tim Laughran, a highly regarded academic and a finance professor at the University of Notre Dame who studies initial public offerings, an investor would have done better in an index fund rather than having invested in a publicly traded IPO. He notes that the problem with IPO companies is that they start out with promise and attention. The IPO has a high price from the start, and much of its future promise is already built into its early stock price.

Well, when all else fails, there is at least history and the tradition of an established company or fund, to help you decide its investment worth. After all, past performance is a matter of public record. If you know how they've done during their history, prediction of how they are *going* to do becomes a matter of simple deduction and trend analysis.

The myth: *Historical performance is a key indicator of future growth.*
The reality: *In the vast majority of cases, history is of almost no benefit in predicting future performance.*

Morningstar, in 1999 with the bull market raging, identified the top-performing fund within each Morningstar equity style box for that calendar year.

However, when those top-performing nine funds were analyzed three years later, *only two* performed better than their respective category averages. The other seven performed *below* their category averages, and five of these had sunk to the bottom quartile.

Clearly, looking backward to determine how to go forward is as dangerous as forging your way up the freeway in rush-hour traffic, looking into your rearview mirror for guidance.

So, let's see where we are so far:

1. No one, no how, no way has the ability to manage or predict the movement of the markets.
2. "Diversification" through mutual funds has limitations: the benefits of "expert" active management do not translate into the growth one would expect.
3. Being up-to-date with the news does not give you information you need to pick winning investments.
4. Picking the minds of the financial press "pros" does not seem to provide a winning investment strategy.
5. The odds of accumulating wealth by getting in on the ground floor of IPOs are miniscule, and the odds against it are great.
6. Past performance as a predictor of future performance is not only unreliable, it can be disastrous.
7. Gambling in the market with high-risk investments is fraught with peril and, on average, likely to result in loss rather than gain.

It would appear that all of the Wall Street wisdom available to investors is flawed, flowered, or fabricated.

So where, you ask, is the gospel—the "good news"—showing you how to secure your long-term investment redemption?

Well, it's simple, it's proven, it's based on pillars of investment research including Nobel Prize-winning economic theory, and it's characterized by the parable in the next chapter.

Chapter II

The Academics of a Sustainable Investment Strategy

or

You Gotta Have Style (and Don't Let It Drift)

It's pretty apparent in chapter 1 that almost all the common wisdom regarding "making it" in the market is flawed. It's flawed because most of that advice is provided by sales persons and institutions with an agenda; they have to sell you a financial product in order to have an income.

Academic research, on the other hand, is subject to *peer review* rather than a brokerage statement. Accordingly, academic research can *afford* to be objective.

We are going to take a simple look at academic research that you can use to provide the greatest long-term returns on your investments. We will examine "modern portfolio theory" and the "capital asset pricing model" both of which won Nobel Prizes in economics. Then we will examine the "Fama-French three-factor model," which expands on the capital asset pricing model.

The Parable of the Agonies

Three actively traded fund managers were returning from a meeting at Paradise Island when their private jet encountered unpredicted, hurricane-like turbulence that ripped the wings off their plane, plunging them into the sea.

As their souls passed to the ether world, the god of the underworld offered them their choices of misery for their eternal damnations: intolerable heat or unbearable cold.

"Heat," said the first one, and he was whisked into a flaming furnace.

"Cold," said the second as he found himself encased in a huge block of ice.

The third manager pondered his answer a bit longer. "Both," he said.

The evil god thought for a second, then, in a heartbeat, the third poor soul found his lower half encased in ice and his upper half inserted into a furnace.

Just a few seconds into their eternal suffering, the first fund manager yelled to the second, "How you doing?"

"Cold as hell," the second replied. "How about you?"

"Hot as hell," the first intoned, as he turned to the third manager. "How about you, Fred? How you doing?"

"Well," Fred replied, "on average, I'm pretty comfortable."

Modern Portfolio Theory—The Value of Diversification

When you stop to consider that "modern portfolio theory" dates back nearly one-half century, perhaps the name should be changed—maybe something like proven portfolio management practice.

First espoused by Harry Markowitz of the University of Chicago in a Nobel Prize-winning paper, modern portfolio theory suggested that *diversification* of appropriate securities would—over the long term—accomplish two goals for investors:

1. reduce risks
2. increase returns

Markowitz contended that appropriate diversification wasn't so much a matter of how *many* securities were included in a portfolio but, rather, the *relationship of each* to the other.

Ideally, appropriately selected securities would complement one another, in that external events that cause one to go down would have the opposite effect upon the other, causing its price to increase.

In so doing, the volatility of the investments was reduced, permitting more consistent and predictable returns over the long term. In addition, since the risk factor was minimized, the overall returns could actually be greater than those for an undiversified or poorly diversified portfolio.

The following chart is a simplistic illustration of how this would work if we ideally had two assets that had "negative correlations," meaning that over the long run, each asset class will provide a reasonable rate of return. However, in the short run, one will win and one will lose. The ultimate result is lower volatility, or risk. This translates into a greater likelihood that more money will be available at the end of your accumulation cycle, when you need it most.

Graphic 1
Opposing Risk-Return Characteristics

Meaningful diversification requires mixing asset classes that have dissimilar performance patterns.

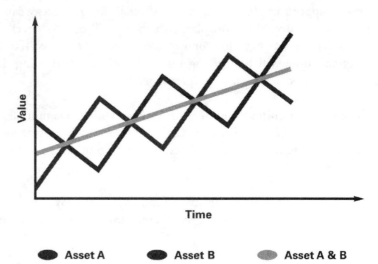

Why is this true? To fully understand this phenomenon, take a closer look at the detailed discussion on lowering volatility in chapter 3. In the "tortoise and hare example," we demonstrate that **even though three portfolios can have the same average annual return, in the end, the dollar amount available in the portfolio with the lowest standard deviation (volatility) is greatest!** The ride might not be quite as fun, but the end result sure is much better!

Think about the implications of this approach for a second. Most people have just one objective in mind when they consider an investment. They only want to buy winners. What Markowitz's Nobel Prize-winning research is telling us is something quite different. Forget about only buying winners—stocks that just go up. You need to select investments based on the fact that when some go up, others are actually going down, and vice versa. This is the basis for a sustainable, long-term investment strategy.

Another way of looking at the relationship between diversification and how well a portfolio performs is to make an analogy to an engine. If the pistons only move up, you won't go anywhere. To have "forward progress," all the pistons must move up and down in an appropriate and sustainable sequence.

If all pieces of your portfolio engine are moving together in lockstep, red flags should be going up all over the place. You can be certain the day will come when they will all retreat in unison too. This creates an unacceptable level of volatility. It will also lead to lower returns over the long run. Not to mention what it does to your gas mileage.

However, as simple as the concept of not putting all your eggs in one basket might appear, implementing a true diversification strategy can be difficult. First, you need a diversification plan (which we will discuss later). Second, you need asset classes that have low or negative correlations—just like the pistons in the engine, some will be moving up while others are moving down, but the net result will be sustainable progress forward.

The problem in implementing this strategy with active mutual funds is something called *style drift*. This is not a fashion blunder such as wearing bell-bottoms to a black-tie affair. However, it is common among active mutual fund and stock managers.

Let's use an example to illustrate fund drift. Let's say a fund you invest in, that is allegedly investing in U.S. small companies, winds up owning midcap stocks.

You might not notice until you start losing money when U.S. small caps are gaining in value. Or let's say you invest in ten mutual funds you thought were properly allocated, and when the market corrects (a nice word for when it goes down), all ten funds go down too.

How can this happen?

One way is that a mutual-fund prospectus can give its manager a wide range of discretion. So even though it may state "small cap" in the name of the fund, a careful reading of the prospectus gives the manager discretion to move out of his original mandate. So while you thought you had a small-cap fund, your fund manager may have decided to make a bet on a different asset class to increase his year-end bonus. Another way "style drift" can occur is if a new manager is hired and decides to change the direction of the fund.

Such changes can occur and have occurred without investors knowing about it until it is too late. In the late '90s, some investors bought five funds in the same fund family not knowing that they owned 95 percent of the same stocks! In the authors' experiences, this was very common and ruinous to many individuals who tried to diversify on their own. One more way Wall Street and greed destroy portfolios.

Capital Asset Pricing Model (CAPM)—The One-Factor Model

Identifying the relationship between risk and return, the CAPM earned William Sharpe a Nobel Prize in economics.

His model provides for two types of risk:

- Market risk—is the risk inherent to capital markets. Sometimes referred to as "beta," such risk *cannot* be overcome by diversification with securities.
- Nonmarket risk—is firm specific, that is, it is risk unique to specific companies. This risk *can* be overcome through diversification.

Once the above is assumed, Sharpe's model essentially states that capital markets are efficient, and therefore, investors cannot find high-risk or high-reward opportunities. Further, stock prices are all in equilibrium in that, at any given time, the value is determined when the price at which a number of people wish to sell is the same as that at which a comparable number of people wish to buy.

Essentially, Sharpe's model shows that you can't eliminate *company* risks by picking individual stocks. Instead, you can only minimize company risks by not concentrating your portfolio in any one sector. What you are left with is *market* risk which is "beta" and can be achieved by investing in an index fund.

In other words, all stocks are fairly priced. So when you turn on the TV and the guru of the moment tells you the market is undervalued or overvalued, think about the foolishness of this position. On the day you saw the guru, about 1.5 billion shares traded on an open and free market and determined the market price at the close. So 1.5 billion shares voted and determined a price, and according to the guru, they are wrong, and he is right. The sheer chutzpah!

Most important, Sharpe also concluded that investors are not really *rewarded* for taking on company or industry risk, providing yet another rationale for a carefully diversified portfolio.

To substantiate the worth of Sharpe's model, it has been consistently shown that very few investors have ever received returns equal to the market as a whole, and fewer yet have actually beat it.

Let us be clear as to what this means in plain English. Someone won a Nobel Prize for proving that one *cannot* be adequately rewarded for picking stocks! Can you imagine the scene at a cable business channel if they interviewed Dr. Sharpe?

> Announcer: So, Professor Sharpe, what stocks and sectors do you recommend?
> Dr. Sharpe: Well, you know (John, Bob, Tina, Dan), I won a Nobel Prize for proving you should not *pick* stocks but, rather, you need to *diversify* over the entire market.
> Announcer: Uh, but if that's true, Dr. Sharpe, we do not have a show.
> Dr Sharpe: Go figure.

OK. So if *you* and *we* cannot pick stocks, maybe the *professional managers* of active mutual funds *can*. After all, these are the people who are paid millions of dollars to beat the market.

Let's see if history and data support Dr. Sharpe or the funds' managers. If we compare active mutual-fund performance against the S&P 500 index for a ten-year period, from March 31, 1994, to March 31, 2004, it's clear that the vast majority of managed funds failed to achieve the levels of performance one would expect. The results of the study are shown in the chart below:

Total Universe: Large Cap Blend Funds	1,545 Funds
Large Cap Blend Funds with Ten-Year History	266 Funds
Average Rate of Return for Large Cap Blend Funds	9.83%
Average Rate of Return for S&P 500 Index for Ten Years	11.68%
Number of Funds Exceeding S&P 500 Index Rate of Return	38 Funds

Source: Morningstar

Think about it: Over a ten-year period, a total of 1,545 actively managed large cap funds existed. Of these, 266 were in existence throughout the ten years of the study. Of all the funds in the study, only thirty-eight actively managed funds *exceeded* the average return of the S&P 500 during that time—a mere 14 percent of those whose existence spanned the ten-year study period and less than 2.5 percent of all of the funds.

Of course, you might consider merely buying one of those thirty-eight funds that were winners. After all, everyone tells you to look at track records in picking the right fund.

The myth: *Track record is a predictor of future performance.*
The reality: *History shows the best performing funds in one decade (in the '70s, '80s, and '90s) are not the best performers in the following decade.*

Ask yourself this question: "Why does the front page of every mutual-fund prospectus state that past performance is no guarantee of future results?" Answer: because it is TRUE!

What makes the results of this analysis even more staggering is that we have completely ignored the tenure of fund managers and the effect management changes have on a fund's performance. This analysis begs the question: If you cannot *beat* the index, why not just *buy* the index (more on this later)?

Investors always want to know how much a portfolio will earn. In the world of investment professionals, this is called the expected return of a portfolio. To answer this question, we must understand the concept of an "equity premium." This means, in plain English, how much more do equities have to earn over a safe investment such as T-bills in order for you to take the risk of losing principal? Using an equity premium estimate of 6.5 percent over the T-bill rate, and a T-bill rate of 2 percent, one would expect equities to grow at 8.5 percent per annum. If your risk tolerance indicated you needed a portfolio of 50 percent equities and 50 percent bonds, the expected return would be the weighted average of these numbers. In this case, it is relatively simple.

$$(50\% \times 2\%) + (50\% \times 8.5\%) = 5.25\%$$

The question is will this expected return meet your financial goals even though it is consistent with your risk tolerance? There is no easy answer, and like most thing in life, there is a compromise that needs to be reached between your emotions and your goals.

The Three-Factor Model—The Return of the "Return"

Clearly, the first two concepts in this chapter aim to increase returns by reducing (not eliminating) risks. But doesn't doing so also compromise returns? And if so, is the additional safety worth it?

Kenneth French and Eugene Fama defined a model which suggested that only three criteria were responsible for more than 96 percent of the variability of a portfolio:

1. The expected returns for "equities" (stocks wherein you actually own a piece of the pie) are higher than for fixed income "securities" (such as Treasury bills)—the equity premium.
2. "Value stocks" (based on the ratio of book value to market capitalization) have a higher expected return than "growth stocks" (the higher-priced book value to market capitalization spreads).
3. Measured by market capitalization, smaller companies provided higher expected returns (on average) than larger company stocks. (They are also riskier.)

Graphic 4
Size and Value Effects are Strong Around the World

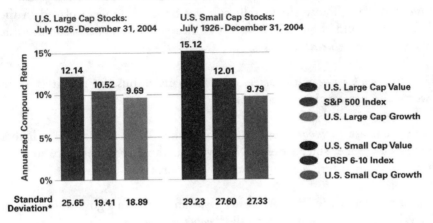

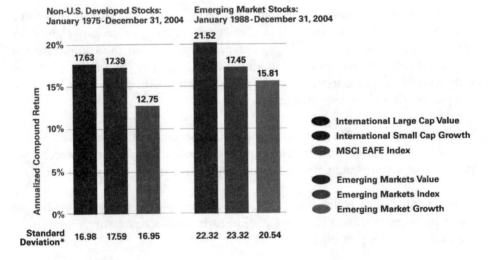

Source: Dimensional Fund Advisors (DFA). In U.S. dollars. Value and Growth data courtesy of Fama/French. International Small simulated by DFA prior to 4/86 portfolio inception. Emerging Markets simulations from countries in the International Finance Corporation Global Universe. Simulations are value weighted within each country then equal weighted across all countries. See pages 17 and 18 for sources of data.

*Annualized number is presented as an approximation by multiplying the quarterly number by the square root of the number of periods in a year. Please note that the number computed from annual data may differ materially from this estimate.

The chart illustrates how French and Fama came to these conclusions. Starting in 1926 (for domestic markets), they created two new asset classes for large companies. Taking all stocks in the S&P 500, they divided them into a *growth*— and *value-asset* class. Those stocks selling *above* book value were placed in the *growth-asset* class, and those selling at a significant discount *below* book value were placed in the *value-asset* classes.

Simply stated, *book value* is the assets of a company minus the liabilities, or in other words the net worth of a company.

Companies that are *in favor* (the market loves them) typically sell at a higher price than book value, since investors believe that these companies are worth a premium based on future earnings and growth potential.

The opposite is companies that are *out of favor* and sell at a significant discount to book value. These are sometimes called *value companies*.

The result of the Fama-French research—dividing stocks into growth and value classes—is startling: The return of the "value-asset class" over seventy-eight years beats the market by almost 1.5 percent per annum. Even more impressive is what happened in the world of small companies. Small companies are those with a market capitalization representing the bottom fifty percentile of all U.S. companies, traded on any exchange.

Small companies provide a higher return than large companies albeit with higher risk. Value companies outperform growth companies by almost 5 percent per annum over seventy-eight years—a record no active manager can approach.

So Fama and French concluded that just three factors—(1) market risk, (2) style (value beats growth), and (3) size (small beats large)—account for 96 percent of the variability of a portfolio!

Even more interesting, not only does this work in the U.S. markets, but it appears to be a worldwide phenomenon. These three factors are based on research from over seventy-eight years of market data rather than the opinions of a manager with a ten—or fifteen-year track record.

Why does this work? The best explanation is an analogy with loans. If a large stable company wishes to borrow money from a bank, it will typically pay a significantly lower rate than a company with a weak balance sheet. Creditors want to be compensated for higher lending risk.

This same effect explains why riskier (i.e., value) and smaller companies (size) will provide a higher expected return than large stable companies. Yet the common wisdom is to buy large well-run companies in order to get a better return. The data just does not support this position.

By implementing Fama and French's strategy, one can increase the expected return of a portfolio by 2 percent to 3 percent over the market return, otherwise known as the beta. For you, this will provide a significant increase in the ultimate value of your portfolio. This is something few active managers have ever achieved.

To do this, though, you need to do something that is the antithesis of what every advisor and financial publication has led you to believe; you need to tilt your portfolio away from blue chip companies and toward smaller value-oriented companies. Do you still need large well-run companies in your portfolio? Absolutely, but not to the exclusion of these other asset classes.

So how do you go about implementing this strategy? How can you invest in the market using asset classes based on the three factors?

Dimensional Fund Advisors, an institutional investment company, has taken the Fama-French research and developed asset-class-specific mutual funds that are based on the three-factor model. These funds are style consistent and have extremely low internal costs and turnover. They are passively managed, meaning, if a security fits a certain asset class, it is included without regard to the opinion of any manager or the financial condition of the company.

To understand the benefits based on this approach, we have included the following matrix of asset classes. These asset classes represent specific parts of the market that have low relative correlations, meaning they move in the market without much of a connection to the factors influencing the other asset classes listed.

Asset Class Average Annual Returns and Historical Events—Random Asset Class Performance

Iran/Iraq War Escalates	U.S. Becomes a Debtor Nation	Bombing of Libya	Record-Setting Market Decline	Bank Failures Peak	Junk-Bond Debacle	Iraq Invades Kuwait	Recession in U.S.; Soviet Union Dissolves	Los Angeles Riots	Midwestern U.S. Floods	Fed Raises Interest Rates Six Times
1984	1985	1986	1987	1988	1989	1990	1991	1992	1993	1994
21.85%	67.29%	70.16%	70.55%	33.48%	31.49%	9.10%	49.01%	34.98%	47.17%	12.42%
13.10%	60.11%	69.43%	31.22%	30.80%	29.34%	9.09%	42.96%	28.30%	33.49%	8.84%
11.17%	56.17%	50.10%	24.64%	28.30%	27.46%	-3.17%	40.28%	19.80%	26.48%	5.30%
10.08%	32.17%	24.79%	6.42%	26.01%	24.69%	-15.61%	34.76%	16.05%	25.85%	2.46%
9.39%	31.37%	20.27%	6.20%	24.05%	16.32%	-15.97%	30.12%	7.31%	18.86%	1.29%
7.60%	31.02%	18.47%	5.23%	23.66%	11.51%	-16.77%	15.94%	6.00%	15.46%	1.21%
7.39%	27.90%	12.10%	3.87%	16.81%	10.54%	-20.17%	12.28%	5.19%	13.66%	0.70%
6.27%	13.50%	8.92%	-4.86%	14.52%	9.60%	-22.55%	11.00%	-3.11%	9.61%	-1.34%
3.72%	11.85%	7.13%	-6.10%	7.40%	8.90%	-23.44%	8.73%	-13.14%	5.40%	-4.54%
-5.54%	10.52%	5.10%	-9.05%	6.20%	6.73%	-26.12%	7.05%	-18.37%	4.41%	-8.39%

Negative Returns were received in the gray area

■ DFA U.S. Large Cap Growth: 12.73%
□ DFA U.S. Large Cap Value: 13.79%
◆ DFA U.S. Small Cap: 11.80%
◇ DFA U.S. Small Cap Value: 14.92%

Dow Tops 4000...and 5000; Maket Too High	Technology Stocks Stumble	Chaos in Asian Markets	Global Economic Turmoil	Fears of Y2K Computer Problems	Internet Bubble Burst	World Trade Center and Pentagon Terrorist Attacks	Corporate Scandals	War in Iraq	Escalating Oil Prices
1995	1996	1997	1998	1999	2000	2001	2002	2003	2004
38.36%	33.84%	33.07%	28.67%	28.50%	28.38%	22.63%	5.30%	59.39%	32.06%
37.08%	22.62%	30.75%	18.21%	25.41%	10.21%	13.17%	4.17%	58.79%	30.91%
30.18%	22.32%	28.13%	14.87%	21.87%	9.01%	12.68%	3.90%	51.50%	28.79%
29.29%	20.22%	24.23%	11.98%	20.78%	6.72%	6.10%	1.91%	49.94%	25.38%
13.05%	17.67%	19.37%	8.20%	16.29%	6.50%	5.75%	-8.51%	35.70%	18.81%
12.07%	7.81%	5.99%	6.50%	13.04%	2.45%	3.85%	-9.27%	35.58%	18.25%
11.49%	7.20%	5.90%	5.68%	4.80%	-0.18%	-10.51%	-14.60%	34.43%	17.86%
8.30%	6.34%	5.51%	-5.54%	4.60%	-5.42%	-12.07%	-14.89%	28.49%	10.72%
7.97%	5.78%	-3.14%	-7.28%	4.59%	-9.25%	-15.25%	-19.12%	1.92%	0.88%
0.48%	2.56%	-23.72%	-15.38%	-1.98%	-14.00%	-20.83%	-22.23%	1.63%	0.73%

- DFA International Large Cap: 11.22%
- DFA International Large Cap Value: 16.07%
- DFA Small Cap International: 13.73%
- DFA Real Estate Equity REITS: 12.81%
- DFA One Year Fixed Income: 6.29%
- DFA Two Year Global Fixed Income: 6.86%

The results are year ending as of 12/31 for the year listed.

*Source-Dimensional Fund Advisors, Inc.
Average Annualized returns are from 1/84 to 12/04.

Asset Class Average Annual Returns and Historical Events*

The above chart illustrates the randomness of asset class performance. Historically, even in or during the significant adverse political and economic events, some asset classes have experienced positive returns. Although this chart cannot predict how asset classes will perform in the future, it does illustrate that not all asset classes react negatively to bad news. The disciplined process of asset allocation and periodic re-balancing is a prudent investment approach in these changeable market environments.

An examination of this matrix shows there are ten asset classes, ranked each year from best to worst performing, over the last twenty years. The lighter boxes separate those that made money each year from those that lost. Each asset class is coded with its own symbol to aid the reader in identifying any patterns or trends, thus, enabling the investor to select the next hot asset class and drop what is sure to be the next cold asset class.

Patterns? Trends? You don't see any patterns or trends? Of course not; there is no way to identify the next hot asset class. Once again, it is folly even to try. If you are an engineer and reading this book, please stop trying to find an algorithm to explain the randomness.

Each asset class has relatively good performance. Additionally, it is obvious that these asset classes move randomly. Trying to predict which asset classes will be next year's winners is impossible. Investors need to own *all* of them.

Unlike an active manager, these asset classes are passively managed. Passive managers don't make selections based on an opinion about the worth of a stock. Rather, passive managers select stocks with regard as to whether they meet the criteria of a particular asset class. This eliminates both the "human factor" and "luck."

So does it really work? Well, we believe we have made the case that with few exceptions (Warren Buffet, Peter Lynch, or David Strulowitz's ninety-three-year-old aunt Tanta Sadie), no active manager has proven that they can beat the market over the long run. So let's look at the long run.

The following chart shows what you would have made investing one dollar in the S&P 500 versus a 100 percent-equity portfolio invested in DFA asset classes.

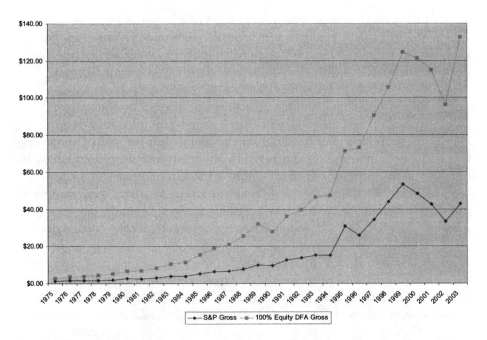

The above table illustrates growth of a dollar invested in the S&P 500 less a .5 percent-management fee versus a dollar invested in a DFA portfolio less a 1 percent-management fee. Even with the additional management fee, the DFA portfolio significantly outperformed the S&P 500 for the period illustrated.

The bottom line: owing to both higher returns and lower fees, an investment with DFA would have yielded approximately twice as much as the S&P 500. **Not only is the overall return higher net of fees 15.89 percent versus 13.1 percent, but the standard deviation (i.e., risk) is lower 14.87 percent versus 16.18 percent.**

So now we have a strategy based on long-term results rather than the track record of a "hot manager." It provides a higher return than the overall market. If this is so great, why doesn't everyone do this? The simple answer is it is not in Wall Street's best interest to promote a low-cost strategy that makes their research irrelevant.

Some investors may conclude that such results may be achieved by merely buying index funds. Although buying index funds is better than betting on an active manager, this is *not* an indexing strategy.

An index is a benchmark to measure the performance of an active manager; as an example, the S&P 500 index represents the top 500 companies in the United States, based on market cap.

An asset class, on the other hand, is composed of a basket of stocks or bonds that is designed to capture a certain incremental return such as the DFA small cap value, which is designed to capture the size and style factor in the Fama-French three-factor model.

Is Ignorance Bliss? The True Cost of Investing With Active Managers

Ignorance may be bliss, but turning a blind eye to the expense of actively managed funds can be costly. As you probably know, active managers attempt to beat benchmarks by selecting mispriced securities and timing the market. They charge investors more for doing this, and these fees reduce returns. What many active investors don't know is that hidden trading costs not reported in a fund's prospectus often create additional drag on performance, further lowering returns.

Aren't these costs reflected in expense ratios? No, and according to a study[1] by the Zero Alpha Group, which examined more than 5,000 domestic equity funds, these funds averaged trading costs 43 percent as large as the disclosed annual expenses. In some instances, unreported trading costs exceeded the funds' annual expense ratios.

These hidden expenses can be difficult to track, as John Bogle suggests in his book Bogle on Mutual Funds: New Perspectives for the Intelligent Investor. The costs represent a combination of brokerage commissions and market impact costs. While brokerage commissions are reported to the Securities and Exchange Commission (SEC) and can be quantified, market impact—the effects of buying and selling on pricing—is more difficult to measure. Stock purchases tend to push prices up, while sales drive prices down.

To account for these factors, Bogle estimates that a trade costs, on average, .6 percent of the amount of the transaction. In order to determine the impact of trading on a fund, he suggests doubling the turnover ratio, then multiplying that figure by .6 percent. So, if a fund has 85 percent turnover, which is average by many standards for actively managed funds, the hidden trading costs using Bogle's method would be 1.02 percent. But remember, this is without taking into account the expense ratio. For funds with higher turnover ratios, such as Janus Mercury, hidden trading costs can be an estimated 2.41 percent. Add to that an expense ratio of 1.12 percent, and the total cost jumps to 3.53 percent.

Using Bogle's method, Charles Schwab compared the annual costs to the investor of typical no-load funds and load funds. Schwab's findings show that with trading

---

[1]   Zero Alpha Group, "Portfolio Transactions Costs at U.S. Equity Mutual Funds," November 2004.

costs, the average cost of no-load funds to the investor is 3.46 percent, slightly lower than the average cost of all funds (3.53 percent) as seen in the chart below.

Fund Name	Expense Ratio %	Trading Costs %	Sales Charge %	Total Costs %
AIM Constellation	1.20	0.54	1.10 [2]	2.84
Alger Small Cap	2.11	1.16	1.00 [3]	4.27
Alliance Balanced Shares	1.32	2.14	0.85 [4]	4.31
Alliance Growth	1.35	0.73	0.85 [4]	2.93
Alliance Growth Investors	1.40	1.15	0.85 [4]	3.40
Alliance Income Builder	2.38	1.04	0.85 [4]	4.27
Alliance International	1.73	1.43	0.85 [4]	4.01
Alliance Quasar	1.83	1.92	0.85 [4]	4.60
Alliance Strategic Balanced	1.40	1.67	0.85 [4]	3.92
Alliance Technology	1.75	0.66	0.85 [4]	3.26
Berger 100	1.48	1.37	0.00 [1]	2.85
Berger Small Co. Growth	1.89	1.31	0.00 [1]	3.20
CGM Capital Development	0.85	3.25	0.00 [1]	4.10
Dean Witter Capital Growth	1.89	0.40	0.20 [5]	2.49
Dean Witter Developing Growth	1.77	1.37	0.20 [5]	3.34
Dean Witter European Growth	2.23	0.74	0.20 [5]	3.17
Dean Witter Natural Resources	1.90	0.71	0.20 [5]	2.81
Fidelity Blue Chip	1.02	2.18	0.60 [6]	3.80
Fidelity Contrafund	1.00	2.82	0.60 [6]	4.42
Fidelity Emerging Growth	1.09	1.22	0.60 [6]	2.91
Fidelity Magellan	0.96	1.44	0.60 [6]	3.00
Fidelity Select Biotechnology	1.59	0.93	0.60 [6]	3.12
Fidelity Select Computers	1.69	2.27	0.60 [6]	4.56
Fidelity Select Health Care	1.36	1.81	0.00 [1]	3.77
Fidelity Trend	0.89	1.75	0.00 [1]	2.64
Founders Special	1.29	3.15	1.00 [3]	4.44
Hancock Special Equity	1.48	0.98	0.00 [1]	3.46
Janus Enterprise	1.23	2.32	0.00 [1]	3.55
Janus Growth Income	1.17	2.34	0.00 [1]	3.51
Janus Mercury	1.12	2.41	0.00 [1]	3.53
Janus Overseas	1.73	2.20	0.00 [1]	3.98
Pasadena Growth	1.60	0.79	1.10 [2]	3.49

[1]   Fund has no front-end or trailing charges.

[2]   Fund has a front-end charge of 5.5 percent, which is 1.1 percent per year.

[3]   Fund has a front-end charge of 5 percent, which is 1.0 percent per year.

[4]   Fund has a front-end charge of 4.25 percent, which is .85 percent per year.

[5]   Fund has a trailing charge of 1 percent in the sixth year, which is 2 percent per year for the period held.

[6]   Fund has a front-end charge of 3 percent, which is .6 percent per year.

George Putnam A	0.91	1.23	1.15 [7]	3.29
George Putnam B	1.66	1.23	1.15 [7]	4.04
Putnam Bal Retired	1.15	1.57	1.15 [7]	3.87
Putnam Global Growth	1.28	0.75	1.15 [7]	3.18
Putnam Investors	0.99	1.64	1.15 [7]	3.78
Putnam New Opportunities	1.88	0.68	1.15 [7]	3.71
Putnam OTC Emerging Growth	1.14	1.39	1.15 [7]	3.68
Putnam Vista	1.07	1.38	1.15 [7]	3.60
Putnam Voyager	1.07	0.78	1.15 [7]	3.00
Scudder Capital Growth	0.98	1.84	0.00 [1]	2.82
Templeton Developing Markets	2.10	0.19	1.15 [7]	3.37
Templeton Global Opportunities II	2.22	0.32	1.15 [7]	3.37
Templeton Small Company Growth	2.11	0.38	1.15 [7]	3.26
Average ALL FUNDS	1.47	1.41	0.66	3.53
Average NO-LOAD FUNDS	1.26	2.19	0.00	3.46

Footnotes: For sales charges we assume a fund is held for five years.
Trading costs are calculated as suggested in the book, Bogle on Mutual Funds, Chapter 10. The method involves doubling the reported annual turnover and multiplying by .6percent. Turnover is the number of dollars of securities sold in a year and must be doubled since the sales lead to purchases with the same money. The .6 percent comes from various sources, including a 1993 study in the Financial Analyst's Journal. The book suggests that this number typically approximates .5 percent to 2 percent of portfolio assets per year, depending on the liquidity of a portfolio's securities.

Source: Palley Needelman

There's more bad news. Taxes. The active investor has to add to this drag on performance the negative tax consequences of funds with high turnover. So, how does a passively managed program compare? In one such program that the authors are familiar with, the average internal charge of a DFA portfolio is .41 percent, and the average advisory fee is 1.11 percent. Add to this Schwab's average trading cost of .10 percent, and total costs average 1.62 percent. This is significantly lower than the true cost of investing in many actively managed funds.

If your goal is to manage your money efficiently, your financial advisor should provide a full disclosure of all fees and transaction costs. Dimensional Fund Advisors (DFA), as a passive manager, minimizes trading costs and, in some cases, has negative trading costs. They achieve this cost-effective result by buying large blocks of stock at a discount from sellers willing to accept a lower price for faster execution. For example, on average, DFA's block purchase price for small cap stock is 3 percent lower than the next day's closing price.

---

[7]   Fund has front-end charge of 5.75 percent which is 1.15 percent per year.

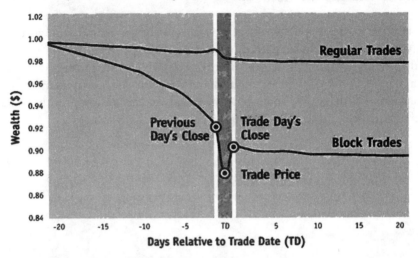

Small Cap Stock Trades (Buys Only) January 1985-December 2003

Dimensional continually monitors its trading advantage. On a quarterly basis, Professor Donald Keim of the University of Pennsylvania's Wharton School of Business measures the value that the firm adds from trading small cap stocks at a discount.

The graph illustrates this "negative trading" effect for DFA. For small company stocks, as a trade date approaches, the price of stock will typically fall to the "Previous Day's Close". The reason for this is that small company stocks usually have few shares change hands on any given day. When word spreads among traders that a large block of stock is being put on the market to sell, buyers drive down the price they are willing to pay for the stock due to the oversupply. The graph illustrates the overall impact of DFA's policy implementation over the period shown and may not represent the results of more recent periods not covered by the data.

DFA takes advantage of this oversupply situation by agreeing to buy the whole block, but only if the seller is willing to take a discounted price, as is illustrated by the "Trade Price" in the graph. In this scenario, that same day, the stock price will stabilize as illustrated by "Trade Day Close". The difference between "Previous Day Close" and "Trade Price" is characterized as negative trading costs. This effect benefits investors in DFA's products, who pay less for shares of stocks purchased. DFA also has patient selling protocols, as they take advantage of selling stocks in small increments over long periods of time to avoid moving the market price in a negative manner. Most active managers do not attempt to generate negative trading costs, either because they are unable to buy "in bulk" or are unwilling to wait to fill a position for their portfolio, and accept higher costs in to complete the order.

For better or worse, a good financial advisor will always remind you what it costs to invest. High fees, hidden trading costs, and high turnover are things you should generally avoid, but are oftentimes part of the package with active management. This can create significant drag on the performance of your investments. With passive management, based on the philosophy that markets are efficient, you can avoid these significant cost disadvantages.

Chapter III

Managing Risks for a
Sustainable Portfolio

Markets may be rational, but we, as investors, have a difficult time being rational about our own money. Our emotions and our reaction to risk can have more impact on our portfolio than the actual investments (see DALBAR chart in chapter 3 under heading: *The Greatest Risk to Your Portfolio—Your Emotions*"). As such, we need to manage risk and understand its effect on us and our portfolio.

The Importance of Asset Allocation

We all know what is most important to "make it in the market"; Pick the right securities, and time your purchases and sales—buy low, sell high. Right?

Wrong, according to a landmark 1994 study by Brinson, Beebower, and Singer, "Determinants of Portfolio Performance II: An Update," 1994. In their study, the respective impacts of various criteria—asset allocation, market timing, security, and others—were enumerated.

The widely accepted study was overwhelmingly consistent in the direction in which it pointed. According to BBC & S, "asset *allocation* is the single most important determinant of portfolio success."

Here is how the various criteria stacked up in terms of their impacts on overall portfolio performance:

Graphic 6

Determinants of Performance – The Importance of Asset Allocation
in Overall Portfolio Performance

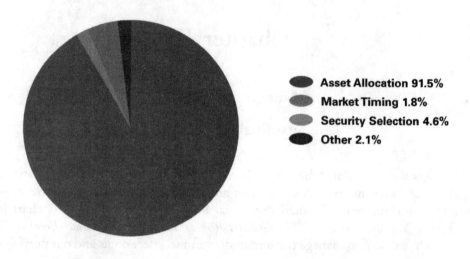

Asset Allocation 91.5%
Market Timing 1.8%
Security Selection 4.6%
Other 2.1%

A common misconception is that portfolio success
depends on selecting the right security and/or timing
the market. Quite the contrary, investment research
actually indicates asset allocation is the single most
important determinant of portfolio success.

Source: Brinson, Beebower & Singer, Determinants
of Portfolio Performance II: An Update, 1994.

In effect, the "holy grail," according to Brinson, Beebower, and Singer, *isn't* a
matter of picking the right stocks or buying and selling them at the right time,
so much as a matter of properly *allocating* your investment money in the *right
proportions* in the *right types* of investments.

This would be just another interesting yet uninspiring illustration of market
tendencies if it were not for the fact that this is exactly how people go about
buying investments. They look at what is (or what moments ago was) hot.

The average Good Samaritan goes about paying taxes, contributing to the United
Way and collecting investment fossils—stocks and mutual funds that at one
time or another demonstrated some type of above-average performance. Will it
do so again? Who knows? Ask the average person why they hold investment X,
and they say it (the stock or fund selected) seemed like a good idea at the time
(market timing).

What the data makes crystal clear is that investment time is *best* spent allocating your dollars over a sensible mix of low-correlation asset classes. Staying the course, no matter what news events or catastrophes occur is paramount to a sustainable strategy.

To be effectively allocated, one needs to be an "investor," not a collector of stocks. If you are watching the overall worth of your investments decline in a declining market, you are *not* properly diversified; you've *collected stocks* rather than *allocating* your investments in the right types of assets.

The most important decision in allocation is how much should be allocated to bonds versus equities. This decision determines how much you will allocate to safe money (bonds—see discussion below for what is a safe bond) and risk (the stock market).

The Parable of the African Explorers and the Big Cat (or: Cheetahs Never Win)

Lost, thirsty, and increasingly hungry, two explorers were wandering the periphery of the Serengeti Plain when a large hungry-looking cheetah suddenly stood up in the grass, no more than twenty yards away, its cruel yellow eyes fixed upon them both.

Without hesitation, the explorer closest to the cat threw down his knapsack and began running away from the hungry predator.

"Stop running, you fool," his companion called out as he pursued his suddenly fleet-footed friend. "We must turn and face the cheetah together. You can't possibly outrun him. He's the fastest animal on earth!"

"I don't have to outrun him," the first explorer yelled from a rapidly expanding distance. "I only have to outrun you!"

To Thy Own Self Be True: Risk Tolerance and Its Impact on a Sustainable Strategy

Everyone handles risk and adversity differently. Just as some tourists feel the security of a bus on a paved road near civilization is preferable to the vulnerability to seeing the interior of Africa on foot, some investors prefer the safety of a particular investment to the grandeur of a high rate of return.

Understanding one's *own* risk tolerance is critical in developing a sustainable investment strategy. Studies have shown that individuals believe they have a higher risk tolerance than they do as is evidenced by the number of people who "bailed" after the recent market debacle. This disparity (between what people *think* they can tolerate and what they *can* tolerate) can cause significant problems in designing a portfolio. What happens if one's need for a certain growth rate is inconsistent with one's tolerance?

If, for example, you need an 8 percent expected return to meet your goals, but your risk tolerance indicates you should have a portfolio that results in only a 6 percent expected return, you have a problem. The dilemma is that if you implement the more aggressive portfolio, it may not be sustainable; you will be tempted to bail out following a downturn. Conversely, if you implement the more conservative portfolio, it will not meet your goals. The resolution of such conflicts requires you to work with an advisor. Most advisors will use a risk-tolerance questionnaire and will incorporate some generally utilized guidelines.

"Time horizon" is one of the key guidelines in deciding how to allocate your investments. The more time you have before you need access to your funds, the more (in theory) you can allocate to equities versus bonds. In other words, if you won't need the money shortly, you can accept greater risk, as—if it declines— you've more time during which it can recover. The first step in allocating your portfolio, therefore, is determining what percentage to allocate to equities. A simple formula is the following:

100 - your age = percent allocable to equities

Using the above formula, if you are age thirty-five, you would allocate 65 percent to equities (100 - 35=65%). While this is only a very simple formula, it is a very good guideline.

But what if you really have reached your financial goals and have more money than you think you will need for the rest of your life? People in this situation often fall into one of two opposing camps:

The first camp wants to aggressively commit a large allocation to equities simply because—irrespective of having reached their financial goals—they believe the race is never over. Unfortunately, this does not make a lot of sense since they are taking a risk that they do not need. To illustrate this point, many retirees over allocated to equities in the '90s and lost good portions of their nest eggs.

The other camp wants *no* market risk and wants *everything* invested in bonds or CDs. Unfortunately; they do not take into account risks from taxes and inflation. In the last fifty years, CDs and T-bills have rarely provided positive after-tax and after-inflation returns.

A simple example illustrates this point: Assume a CD earns 4 percent. If you are in the 30 percent tax bracket your yield is only 2.8 percent after tax, since 1.2 percent (30 percent of your 4 percent earnings) went to the government. Since inflation historically has averaged 3 percent per annum, 3 percent of your total investment is also eaten up by decreased purchasing power. By the time the tax man and inflation have taken their cuts, the real *return* on your 4 percent CD is a *loss* of -0.2 percent! Few individuals can afford to have a portfolio that is 100 percent bonds or fixed income because—in real terms—they are *losing* money.

The issues involved in determining bond-versus-equity ratios for a given portfolio are complicated; they not only involve analytics, but emotions as well. If these are not in balance, it is unlikely your investment strategy will be sustainable.

If we define risk as volatility, we need to understand its affects not only on our emotions but in the ultimate value of our portfolio.

Reduction of Volatility—The Key to It All

Remember the fable of the tortoise and the hare? The hare took off like a rocket but couldn't sustain his pace. At the end, the slow-but-steady tortoise eased by the exhausted bunny, winning the race. Of course, given time to rest, the rabbit would regain his energy, take off like a rocket again, and no doubt surpass the tortoise again.

One would assume that if, *on average*, their speeds were the same, the race would end in a tie. It's analogous to the performance of two investments—one with high volatility and one with low. If both investments—*on average*—yielded the same *annual* return, both would have the same worth at the end of five years, right?

WRONG!

Average returns are not a good indicator of portfolio performance.

Tortoise and Hare Example—A Demonstration of Why It Really Is More Important to Finish the Race, Rather Than Sprint the Fastest!

In the following chart, all three portfolios (A, B, and C) have the same simple average return of 7 percent over the course of five years, so the returns for each sum up to 35 percent.

However, portfolio A has the lowest volatility (as measured by standard deviation) of 1.58 percent while portfolio B has a volatility of 21.39 percent (the larger the standard deviation, the higher the risk, or volatility). So in this case, portfolio B is almost fifteen times more risky than portfolio A. Despite the fact that the average annual percentage returns for both portfolios are the same, portfolio B, with over thirteen times the volatility, fell far short of portfolio A in terms of the actual return.

Portfolio		*A*	*B*	*C*
Year	1	7.00%	20.00%	13.50%
Year	2	8.00%	-20.00%	-6.50%
Year	3	6.00%	-5.00%	1.00%
Year	4	9.00%	35.00%	21.00%
Year	5	5.00%	5.00%	6.00%
Simple Sum		35.00%	35.00%	35.00%
Simple Average Annual Return		7.00%	7.00%	7.00%
Cumulative Return		40.19%	29.28%	37.47%
Annualized Return		6.99%	5.27%	6.57%
Standard Deviation Volatility		1.58%	21.39%	10.69%
Dollar Amount Invested		$100,000	$100,000	$100,000
Dollar Amount at end of Year 5		$140,194	$129,276	$137,474

So back to the hare (B) and the tortoise (A); how do you explain the tortoise's victory? Well, slow and steady really *does* win the race. While the hare was resting (and in some cases, stumbling backward), the tortoise kept right on lumbering forward. Not only did the hare have to make up the time he was resting, he had the additional burden of making up for the time he was stumbling backward.

The return in the above example wasn't decided on the basis of one-year averages—it was determined on a day-by-day ongoing effort on the part of the less volatile fund. Its relatively meager percentage returns continued and were compounded while earnings of the volatile fund were nonexistent at times and actually produced losses.

Let us assume you implement portfolio B, and along come years 2 and 3, with -20 percent and -5 percent losses, respectively. If you bail and sell you never get to year 4 with a positive return. This result is all too common in the collective experience of the authors, and as such, it is a double whammy. Not only does volatility *reduce* return if you maintain the allocation, in reality it *destroys* return because you cannot sustain the risk and get a zero or negative return.

So ultimately, what your portfolio allocation is should be based on your risk tolerance and your goals. Most investors do not truly understand risk. What we perceive as safe may have risks. Furthermore, if we are going to take a risk, we need to know, are we maximizing the return we can achieve for a given level of risk?

The following table is illustrative of this risk and return relationship.

January 1976-October 2004

	100 % Long Term Bonds	70% Equity 30% Bonds	15% Equity 85% Bonds
Annual Return	9.68%	13.99%	9.61%
Ending Value	$1,329,132	$3,910,800	$1,305,584
Annual Standard Deviation	10.81%	10.43%	4.67%

Source: Dimensional Fund Advisors

The importance of this table is not only what it says about your ultimate returns, but also what it tells us about volatility. As we discussed earlier, volatility has important implications to your ability to sustain a portfolio (see risk tolerance) and also on the ultimate return of a portfolio.

Standard deviation is the measure of volatility of a portfolio: The higher the standard deviation, the higher the volatility. So if one were to invest in long-term government bonds in the mistaken belief that this was a safe investment, you could have gotten essentially the same rate return of (9.68 percent) by allocating 15 percent to equities and 85 percent to bonds (short-term) with only one-half the risk!

On the other hand, if you could tolerate the volatility of long-term bonds (std. dev. 10.81 percent), then you could have invested 70 percent in equities and 30 percent bonds (std. dev. 10.43 percent) and earned 13.99 percent (instead of 9.68 percent) with essentially the same level of risk!

The difference in ultimate dollar return is huge.

Rebalancing

Having properly *allocated* your investments consistent with your risk tolerance, you now have to manage the portfolio on a *sustainable* basis. The next step is *rebalancing*.

Rebalancing becomes an important factor in reducing risk and maintaining your portfolio. Since these asset classes move randomly, today's winner—in all probability—is tomorrow's loser.

The concept of rebalancing is simple: Let's assume that you have carefully allocated a $1,000,000 portfolio, into four appropriately low-correlating asset classes, all with equal value ($250,000 each).

Again, remember the most important consideration here is reduction of risks—your selections have been carefully made on the basis that a downturn for one of your selections is complemented by an upturn in a corresponding selection. For this strategy to work, it is essential that the respective balances of the various classes be maintained at the initially selected ratios (25 percent of the total, each, in this example).

Now, of the four asset classes you've selected, let's assume the following: asset class one grows by 20 percent, asset class 2 declines by 10 percent, while asset class 3 and 4 grow by 5 percent each.

	Asset Class #1	Asset Class #2	Asset Class #3	Asset Class #4	Total
Beginning Investment	$ 250,000	$ 250,000	$ 250,000	$ 250,000	$ 1,000,000
Return (%)	20%	-10%	5%	5%	
Return ($)	$ 50,000	$ - 25,000	$ 12,500	$ 12,500	$ 50,000
New Value	$ 300,000	$ 225,000	$ 262,500	$ 262,500	$ 1,050,000

At the conclusion of the investment period above, the allocations have become unbalanced: asset class 1, by virtue of its return, has become heavier than the others. In this simple illustration, $37,500 of asset class 1 will need to be sold off and invested in asset class 2 in order to balance all the classes at $262,500. For most investors, however, this creates a dilemma; why sell off a winner?

Two reasons:

1. As previously demonstrated, because of the randomness and unpredictable nature of asset class returns, today's winners may very likely be tomorrow's underperformers. (See previous **Asset Class Average Annual Returns and Historical Events—Random Asset Class Performance Chart.**)
2. As previously discussed, the avoidance of risk is more important to the long-term growth of the portfolio than the attainment of short-term high returns.

Counterintuitive as it may seem, studies indicate that the discipline of selling off winners in order to rebalance your allocations can reduce portfolio volatility up to 70 percent.

The only dilemma in implementing rebalancing is the authors have never met a client who will unemotionally do this on their own. Why? We all want to buy more winners and not losers. We cannot help ourselves. There must be a gene in our DNA that precludes us from setting our emotions aside and doing what we intellectually know is correct when it comes to love and money.

The Greatest Risk to Your Portfolio—Your Emotions

The following chart from DALBAR illustrates the stock-market returns from 1984 to 2003 versus what individuals actually *earned* in their portfolio. The market earned over 12 percent per annum versus only 2.6 percent earned by the average equity investor. The average investor wasted all that time spent trying to find the right investment. Most investors would be better off with an *average* return rather than trying to beat the market.

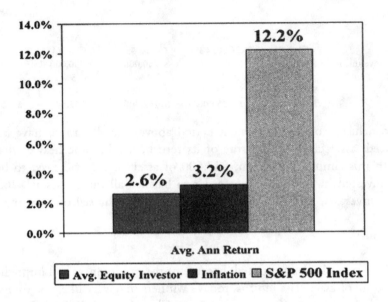

Source: 2003 DALBAR Study-Quantitative Analysis of Investor Behavior

What can possibly explain this poor result? Here is an explanation: Twenty years ago, investors held mutual funds for ten to twelve years. Today, that holding period is down to under two years. Why? Chasing "hot" managers is one answer. It serves as further proof that a sustainable strategy is more important than the current hot stock or fund.

All of that access to financial information leads to only one inevitable conclusion: Current events are not as important to your financial strategy as wisdom and experience. So why are we fascinated with business news, the financial press, and the Internet? There is an old joke that might explain this.

> Man talking to Friend
> Man: I really have a dilemma. My wife thinks she is a chicken and spends
>   all her time in the garage nesting.
> Friend: That is horrible; why don't you take her to a psychologist?
> Man: Because I need the eggs.

Why do we listen to all the financial pornography? We have become addicted to the "eggs." So how do we heal our financial strategy ills?

Just say "no" to eggs.

The Value of Staying Invested—Pitfalls of Market Timing

In chapter 2, we discussed the fact that it is all but impossible to beat the indexes with a "buy low-sell high" strategy—theories suggest and studies prove that it can't be reliably done. But what, exactly, *is* the impact of attempting to "time" your stock *sales* with peaks in the price?

With the exception of an infinitesimally small number of very *lucky* investors, if you are going to derive the benefits of the market, you need to stay fully vested in it, rather than getting in, getting out, getting in, etc.

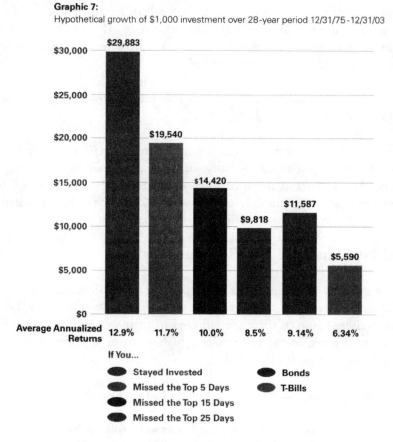

Graphic 7:
Hypothetical growth of $1,000 investment over 28-year period 12/31/75-12/31/03

The chart shows the results of a $1,000 hypothetical investment in the S&P 500 Index on 12/31/75 held through 12/31/03 compared to similar hypothetical investments in the index that were not invested on the days that were the market highs during the period. For comparison, an investment in bonds is shown, represented by the Lehman Aggregate Bond Index. An investment in T-Bills is represented by the Ibbotson U.S. 30-Day T-Bill index. Indices are unmanaged and cannot be purchased directly by investors.

Source of chart data: Ned Davis Research, 12/31/03.

The ramifications are hard to ignore: If you were actively buying and selling given issues over twenty-eight years and failed to own them for the top five days—just four-tenths of 1 percent of that time—your return over that period would have dropped by approximately one-third.

Clearly, without the ability to predict price fluctuations of a given issue, remaining invested is essential to your long-term gain. Getting in and out of the market on any given issue almost ensures that you will miss some very important market peaks.

So let us contrast these facts with what we see and hear every day. The financial guru (always well tailored, love the style) will tell us how it is not quite yet the time to get into the market. The right time to invest is the *next* quarter. Is he so smart (he is, if you ask *him*) that he can *predict* the 1 percent of the time that provides 70 percent of the market return?

The fact is someone will *always* get it right—once. However, getting it right repeatedly is almost impossible.

Even "expert" money managers like Peter Lynch, Michael Price, and Warren Buffet only come along so infrequently that your likelihood of identifying them in advance is a statistical improbability—akin to the preverbal room full of monkeys banging away randomly on typewriters 24/7. Every few hundred years or so, one of the monkeys *may* write a page of Shakespeare!

Stirred Not Shaken: The Role of Bonds

Bonds are essential to stabilizing a portfolio: Their performance is more stable, and risks tend to be lower compared with equities. Although minimal, bonds *do* carry some risks; however, these are reflected in their values at maturity. Higher risk bonds of a given initial value offer a higher return at maturity than lower risk bonds of the same initial value.

There are two primary forms of risks inherent in bonds:

- **Credit risk**—The risk that a bond issuer will default can be low but is, nevertheless, present.
- **Interest rate risk**—As interest rates go up, the risk associated with a given bond issue increases and is reflected in the bond's declining market value.

Investors tend to err in the length of terms in which bonds are purchased. Since longer term bonds are more speculative than shorter term bonds, they offer higher rates of return at maturity. Accordingly, many investors tend to purchase these longer maturing instruments.

However, the additional return is minimal and—relative to the increased risk—is generally not worth it.

In the following chart, the blue line represents the annualized compound returns of bonds at maturity. The lowest returns are for those bonds with the shortest maturities—one-month T-bills in this example. Going from the shortest maturities to the longest (twenty-year government bonds), the rates of return grow from approximately 6 percent to approximately 7.5 percent.

The purple line indicates risk as measured by standard deviation. Standard deviation is (effectively) the amount by which the market value of a bond deviated from the average during its life—greater deviation reflects greater risk.

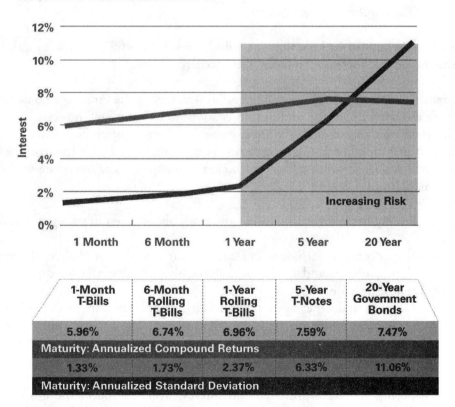

Risk/Reward of Various Bond Maturities

	1-Month T-Bills	6-Month Rolling T-Bills	1-Year Rolling T-Bills	5-Year T-Notes	20-Year Government Bonds
	5.96%	6.74%	6.96%	7.59%	7.47%
Maturity: Annualized Compound Returns					
	1.33%	1.73%	2.37%	6.33%	11.06%
Maturity: Annualized Standard Deviation					

Source: Dimensional Fund Advisors Quarterly January 1964 to June 2004.

As you can see, tying one's funds up in longer term maturities does not have a significant impact upon increasing returns; it does, however, substantially increase the risks.

Yet investors consistently purchase bonds having twenty—and thirty-year maturities. There appear to be two reasons for this:

1. Investors fight for yield, and normally, this means buying longer maturity and/or lower quality bonds, and
2. Brokers make far more money selling longer maturity bonds.

Many investors would argue that number 2 above would not apply to them as there was no commission listed when a given bond was purchased. There are, again, only two likely reasons for this:

1. The broker is willing to work for free (remember the myth of the altruistic Wall Street professional); or,
2. The commission was hidden.

As few (or any) of us know anyone willing to work for free, it's safe to assume that number 2 above is the more likely scenario. How?

Many times, brokers will sell bonds out of inventory of the brokerage house and mark the bond up, so the commission is not obvious—this will, however, reduce the yield over the term of the investment. The largest markups occur on the longest maturing bonds. Also, brokerage houses often buy bonds in large blocks at *discounted* rates, which add to the houses' profits when the bonds are sold on the market.

The following are some things to be concerned about when investing in bonds:

- Bonds come in all flavors and can be quite complex. We believe that one should understand credit risk. Remember today's AAA credit can be tomorrow's Enron.
- GNMAs and other agency bonds such as FNMAs can be complicated investment instruments. Although they are high quality, you may not get what you bargained for. Let's take GNMAs, a favorite of brokers and mutual-fund complexes, as an example. In a GNMA, you are the opposite end of the mortgage relationship. This means a pool of borrowers are paying you back principal and interest over the life of the mortgage. Remember, when interest rates go up, all bond prices go down. But let's

assume you purchase your GNMA in a high interest rate market and rates go down. Well, with most bonds, you would have a gain. But look what happens with GNMAs, the borrower will refinance his or her home as interest rates go down, so you never got to lock in those high rates. This is not a good deal.

- Investors often purchase bonds from brokers then wish to shorten their maturities. This requires them to sell the bonds prior to maturity. They rely on their brokerage statement to provide them with an estimate of what the bonds are worth. Unfortunately, with the exception of treasuries, the prices listed on one's statements are *only* estimates. When someone *does* liquidate, they may find their bonds worth 5 percent or *lesser* than the estimate.

- In the opinions of many qualified investment advisors, the bonds portion of the portfolio is the safe portion of the portfolio. It should avoid strategies that attempt to predict interest rates or increase yield by extending maturity.

- The market in treasury bonds is larger than the daily trading volume of the NY Stock Exchange. The Federal Reserve only controls interest rates over the short term. What this means is although the fed can have an effect on long bond rates, it is really the market that controls interest rates. Attempting to predict the long-term direction of interest rates is as difficult—and as fruitless—as predicting the direction of the stock market.

- What you earn on a bond is not the quoted yield; it is a factor of what you paid for a bond. One can buy bonds above or below their face value (the amount to be repaid to the investor at maturity). If you buy a bond for more than its face value, the difference is called the premium. If you buy it for less, the difference is called a discount (isn't finance fun and logical?).

As We Continue . . .

Let's review again what we've established so far in this book:

To begin, we discussed the reasons why conventional Wall Street wisdom almost assures financial failure—

- Wall Street salespeople are *not* being paid to ensure your financial success—they are paid to sell their *product du jour*.
- The economy is far too complex for *anyone* or *any institution* to be able to predict its long-term oscillations.
- Lacking the ability to do the above, putting all or most of one's eggs in one investment basket is inviting catastrophe
- Although (fees notwithstanding) mutual funds would appear to be a great way to get away from having all your eggs in one basket, *actively managed* funds have, on average, underperformed the market as a whole.
- The "knowledge" obtained from the general media is woefully inadequate to permit winning investment decisions to be made.
- The financial pornography proffered by the "sophisticated and informed" business press, is dead wrong in many cases.
- Initial public offerings of stocks (IPOs) are generally overvalued by the time they become available, due to all the hype surrounding them.
- History does not provide a means of predicting future market actions
- High risk does *not* equal high reward—in fact, on average, it's just the opposite.
- High returns are not the key to your investment growth, reduction of volatility is.

Further, we discussed those pillars of investment that *are* proven methodologies for a winning investment strategy—

- Modern portfolio theory—the value of diversification
- Capital asset pricing model (CAPM)—the one-factor model
- The three-factor model—increasing the expected return of an asset
- Effective asset allocation

- Reduction of volatility—the key to it all
- Rebalancing—essential to avoiding volatility
- The value of staying invested-pitfalls of market timing
- The role of bonds

Following the advice provided so far will maximize the growth of your investment wealth.

But growing wealth is only *part* of the story; the other part is ensuring that your accumulated wealth lasts at least as long as you do. To do this, planning your retirement, and protecting your wealth from confiscatory income and estate tax laws, long-term health costs, and potential third-party litigation is essential. In the next several chapters, we will discuss how you can protect and transfer your wealth while minimizing these risks.

Some of these risks can be transferred to an insurance company. However, certain types of liability may not be coverable by insurance, or the insurance costs may be prohibitive. Accordingly, as we continue, we describe the basics of asset protection.

On the other side of the equation, estate taxes can be reduced with proper planning, which we describe later. However, depending on when you die and if your estate is large enough, you may never be able to eliminate estate taxes unless you are willing to leave your money to charity.

Your qualified plan and/or IRAs offer great vehicles for savings but may be subject to both estate and income taxes resulting in taxes as high as 70 percent. Accordingly, we discuss how to designate beneficiaries for your IRA and qualified plan in order to reduce your beneficiaries' overall tax liabilities.

Of course, these chapters are merely intended as overviews of extremely complicated topics that are subject to change because of new tax or case law. One needs to sit down with their tax professional and lawyer to discuss their individual needs.

Section II

Protecting Your Wealth

Chapter IV

Planning for Your Retirement

The Parable of Saving for a Rainy Day (When the Weatherman Is Rarely Accurate)

Two aged derelicts were seated on a curb one cold Chicago night, in an early winter rain, sharing a bottle of muscatel. "How'd you get here?" the first asked the second.

"Hedonism," the second replied. "I made a pretty good buck during my day but wasted it all pursuing the pleasures of wine, women, and song. If I had it to do over again, I wouldn't have wasted it on the women and the song. What about you?" he continued, taking a deep drink.

"Well," replied the first, "I've been on the street for three years now. I started a business as a young man; worked hard and well at it; married a beautiful, loving, faithful woman; sent our two sons to Harvard; and saved and invested my entire life for retirement."

"In fact," he continued, "I had accumulated such a fortune I was able to retire at age fifty-five, with more than enough assets to last me until I was one hundred, even if I spent every last cent I'd accumulated."

"Wow," exclaimed the second. "What went wrong? Family tragedy? Market collapse? You planned everything and did everything right. What could have gone wrong?"

"I turned 103 yesterday," replied the first.

The Fallacy of "Spend Down" Retirement Planning

Traditionally, retirement planning was built around a "spend down" strategy. The goal of such a strategy was to accumulate enough assets by retirement age that if some amount were spent each year, these retirement assets would last a given number of years (depending upon one's life expectancy). By its very definition, such a spend-down strategy had to be defined in terms of a dollar amount for the value of the assets, divided by the dollars per year over which they would be depleted.

But such a strategy ignores too many factors to provide a valid plan for your twilight years. Let's consider just a few:

1. *How long will you live?* In our own lives, most of us look back at our parents and grandparents for our concepts of normal life expectancies. In doing so, many of us who are of sufficient age to be concerned about retirement today, see '60s, '70s, or even '80s to be a normal life span.

Yet, according to The Annuity 2000 Mortality Table from the Society of Actuaries, if you and your spouse live to be sixty-five, there is a 60 percent chance one or the other of you will live to be ninety . . . and a 33 percent chance one of you will live to be ninety-five!

And keep in mind that with each passing year of improved medical technology, these numbers are constantly increasing.

2. *Will you, your spouse, or loved ones who may become dependent upon you remain healthy?* No health plan or combination of private insurance, Medicare, and Medicaid will provide 100 percent of what you may need. Extraordinary health care requirements, debilitating illness, and similar burdens can rapidly deplete even the most substantial assets. The prospect of nursing home care, just by itself, opens a fresh can of worms when considering your requirements.

Of even more impact, what if one of your *descendants*—a son, a daughter, or a grandchild—faced a potentially fatal or catastrophic illness without the benefit of health insurance. What would you do? If you're like many of us, you would do whatever is necessary to save or diminish the suffering of your loved one, paying for it from your own assets if necessary, while suffering irreparable damage to your own financial security.

3. ***Market volatility.*** No one is immune to market volatility. As a case in point, in the year 2001, the average 401(k) plan balance for persons in their '60s fell approximately 9 percent.

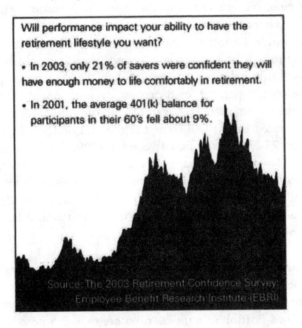

Will performance impact your ability to have the retirement lifestyle you want?

• In 2003, only 21% of savers were confident they will have enough money to life comfortably in retirement.

• In 2001, the average 401(k) balance for participants in their 60's fell about 9%.

Source: The 2003 Retirement Confidence Survey, Employee Benefit Research Institute (EBRI)

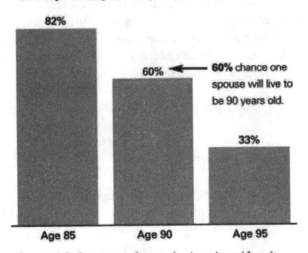

Life Expectancy for 65 year old couple

82%
60%
60% chance one spouse will live to be 90 years old.
33%

Age 85   Age 90   Age 95

Source: Life Expectancy for couples (a male and female age 65) and a single male age 65, calculated using The Annuity 2000 Mortality Table (The Society of Actuaries.)

Such swings in the market can literally decimate your assets and retirement income practically overnight.

4. ***Withdrawal risks.*** No one knows exactly how much income will be required at retirement. There is, however, a substantial risk that—no matter what that amount would be today—the income you will need at the time you actually *do* retire will be substantially greater than it would be now. Many investors mistakenly believe that at retirement, an investment portfolio can generate 6 percent, 7 percent, or 8 percent income annually for many years and sustain their principal. For example, a study conducted by Ibbotson Associates[8] revealed that if you retired at the end of 1972 (right before the bear market of '73-'74) at age sixty-five, with $500,000 saved for retirement, and withdrew 5 percent of that each year—that is used your accumulated savings to create an annual income stream of $25,000—you would have run out of money at age eighty-seven. If you withdrew at a 7 percent rate, with a minimum annual income stream of $35,000, you would have run out of money after only twelve years!

Beliefs about portfolio-income potential and reality have totally different conclusions. If one wanted a 95 percent probability of not running out of money during retirement, most analysis indicates that that the maximum withdrawal rate from a diversified portfolio should be no more than 3.5 percent to 4 percent of initial principal adjusted for inflation!

Speaking of inflation—according to a bureau of labor statistics report published in 2003 and covering the year 2001, the average cost of essentials for a household in which the head of the household was between fifty-five and sixty-four years of age was $35,016. It is quite conceivable that the cost of those same items in fifteen years will be more than twice that.

If so, will you need $70,000 per year? Will you *have* $70,000 per year? And if so, for how long?

Turning Assets into Income

Faced with the possible assaults of lengthened longevity, the high costs of illness and disability, the uncertainty of market volatility, and probable impact of

---

[8]   *High Withdrawal Rates Erode Retirement Portfolios Fast.* Assumes portfolio is invested 50 percent in the S&P 500, 50 percent in five-year U.S. government bonds—assumes reinvestment of income, no transaction costs or taxes.

inflation, ensuring the *continuation* of your assets—and not simply the *amount* of them—is essential to ensuring continuation of your retirement income.

With the amount of retirement income you may need uncertain, and with the future value of your assets unpredictable, it is clear that the protection of your assets takes on increasing importance over the accumulation of them.

A historical perspective is essential to understanding the new realities of retirement planning. Back in the 1960s, many Americans retired with "defined benefit" pensions that provided them with a fixed monthly income, sometimes referred to as defined benefit plans. But there were fundamental problems with the concept of pensions as they existed then. Among these was the fact that ongoing inflation continually reduced the value of the fixed amount benefits paid to pensioners. Further, the high costs of pension plans to employers inhibited their ability to compete against a rising tide of foreign competition, by tying up large amounts of capital for future pension needs.

Throughout the '80s, to combat the shortcomings inherent in structured pension plans, companies shifted away from company-funded pensions to 401(k) plans. For the employee, the benefits included the freedom (to some degree) to select the level of contribution, the freedom to select where that contribution would be invested (from a range of investment types), and the fact that—in many cases—matching funds from the employer were provided. The icing on the cake for employees was the fact that their contributions were 100 percent tax deferred, reducing their current income taxes and, in many cases, dropping them into a lower tax bracket.

For employers, 401(k)s allowed them to reduce employment costs and reduce their long-term obligations, freeing up capital and permitting them to better compete against increasing foreign competition.

An additional benefit of 401(k)s included the fact that—over a wide range— they were inflation resistant. Inflation tended to be reflected in the rising values of the stocks and mutual funds the employees had selected.

Ironically, 401(k)s may have contributed to—and benefited from—the bull stock market of the 1990s. Business capital, freed up by decreased pension set-asides, helped fuel business expansion. At the same time, 401(k) funds began flooding the markets via contributions, many of which went into mutual funds. The net result was an unprecedented increase in stock investment and prices of those stocks, forcing prices higher and attracting new investments to the market.

Unfortunately, there was a pitfall looming: all this occurred just as 401(k)s were becoming increasingly popular, and first-time investors were crowding into the market. The result was that many 401(k) investors had a complete disregard for the realities of the markets' inevitable downturns and invested accordingly. The diversification of their investment selections took the backseat to the notion that they had to put their "safe" retirement savings "somewhere." This is reflected in the DALBAR study which showed that, from 1984 until 2003, while the S&P 500 index grew by 12.6 percent annually, the average annual return for a mutual-fund investor was only 2.6 percent!

[Ed. note: Don't worry about the funds' agents and managers—they still got paid]

It's important to understand this historical perspective for two reasons:

1. The expectations of the value of 401(k) and IRA retirement accounts were largely developed during an investment period that was atypical of the markets. Many investors, therefore, had (and continue to have) unrealistically high expectations for these devices.
2. The markets *are* volatile and, therefore, so are the returns of retirement plans dependent upon them.

In view of the likelihood of longer life, the threat of extended-care illness, market volatility, and withdrawal risks, a complete, spend-down retirement strategy places your "golden year" financial security at great risk. Further, if you are dependent upon the gyrations of the market to provide for you during your retirement, you are placing yourself in even greater jeopardy.

For these reasons, it is essential that your retirement strategy is built not upon the accumulation and systematic depletion of assets, but upon securing for yourself a sustainable, *ongoing income*. This "retirement income strategy" focuses on balancing a spend-down of assets with guaranteed income sources. The result is a higher level of security or "peace of mind" that you will not run out of money (especially if your withdrawal rate is higher than 3.5 percent to 4 percent as mentioned above), and a greater opportunity for your remaining savings and investments to overcome the threats to your retirement security.

The Role of Income Annuities

To balance guaranteed income sources with a spend-down strategy, we have to look beyond traditional investment tools. The concept of an income annuity is really quite simple. In exchange for a lump-sum deposit into an income annuity account or contract, the annuity provides you with an ongoing income stream that is guaranteed to continue for the rest of your life. Like a pension or Social Security, the check arrives in the mail month after month after month. Pretty simple, right? Apparently not!

Over the years, no single financial tool has been more maligned than the annuity. Unfortunately, the financial press and media business experts alike have demonstrated a lack of understanding and/or a bias against these effective tools. Part of the problem lies in the many different types of annuities, from deferred or immediate to fixed or variable. A simple Internet search for "annuity" came up the following "pearls of wisdom":

> **March 2005,** *MSN Money.* "Consider annuities—but as a last resort." By Terry Savage.

> **August 2004, CBS Market Watch.** "The good, the bad, the annuity." By Andrea Coombes.

> **February 2004,** *MSN Money.* "The worst retirement investment you can own." By Liz Pulliam Weston.

If you read these headlines, would you bother reading the article? Probably not. However, each of these respected authors either in the above articles or in later writings promoted the benefits of the lifetime income streams that income annuities provide!

Beyond the simple differences in types of annuities, there are several other items that are important to note about income annuities that may partly explain the negative bias from the financial press.

Income annuities require assumptions about life expectancy. Who makes life-expectancy calculations? Insurance companies. And in the past, the insurance industry has often been its own worst enemy, creating negative reaction in the press and the court of public opinion. In addition, income annuities' most important benefit is providing an income stream that cannot be outlived. It is an *income* tool, not an investment tool. Finally, the guarantee of lifetime income is "subject to the claims-paying ability" of the insurance company. In English, this means that you should select an income annuity from a company that is on sound financial footing.

Utilized appropriately, annuities are an essential part of your retirement-income strategy, providing you with a balance between the spend down of assets and guaranteed income sources.

To illustrate the appropriate use of an income annuity, consider the situation of a seventy-year-old couple, with $450,000 in their retirement fund, current annual income needs of $40,000, and $18,000 per year in Social Security benefits. The spend down of their retirement assets would require them to take $22,000 out of their retirement portfolio the first year. "Normal" inflation could be expected to expand their income needs by 3 percent per year. To further complicate the picture, as noted earlier, there is approximately a one-in-three chance that at least one of them will live to at least age ninety-five.

Annual Expenses & Portfolio Balance

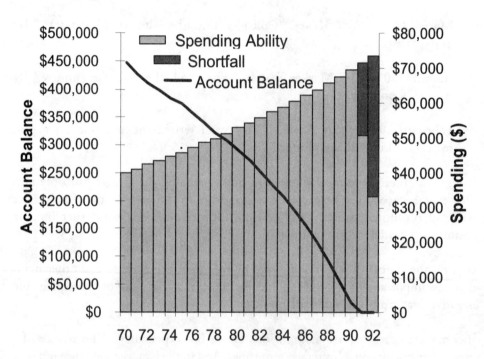

Spending ability shows $40,000 increasing 3 percent annually. Account balance is calculated by simulating $3,000 market scenarios showing the results with a 95 percent probability of success in those scenarios.

Income annuities, however, can reduce the spend down of these retirees to the point that the likelihood is that—not only will they not run out of income, but they will leave behind an inheritance rather than burdening their family. Again, an *income* tool, not an investment tool.

Consider the following illustration, in which the same couple with a $450,000 portfolio, a beginning income requirement of $40,000 per year, of which $18,000 is provided by Social Security, purchases a $250,000 single premium immediate annuity for twenty years certain and life thereafter:

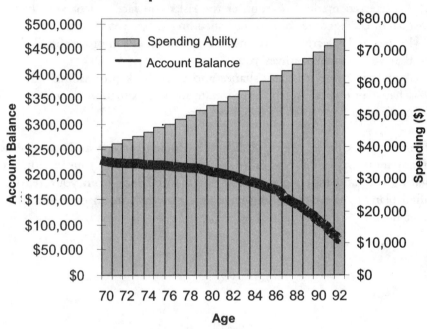

Estimated income based on a $250,000 single premium immediate annuity for a seventy-year-old couple for twenty years certain and life thereafter. All guarantees are based on claims-paying ability of the insurer.

With the annuity paying $18,000 per year and Social Security paying $18,000 per year, the couple's spend down of their portfolio decreases from $22,000 per year to a mere $4,000 per year.

At that rate, not only will the life of their portfolio be extended, but the couple will have a guaranteed income of $36,000 annually (between the annuity and Social Security), as long as they live (assuming the claims-paying capability of the insurance company continues).

So let's review what we have learned:

1. You face very specific and real risks during retirement—outliving your money, long-term illness, market fluctuations, and withdrawing too much money from your "nest egg."
2. Planning on simply spending down your assets as the sole means of providing for your retirement has proven to be a very risky strategy.
3. A preferred method to counter the risks you face is a balance between guaranteed income sources and spending down your assets.
4. Proper and effective use of income annuities will improve the likelihood that your money outlives you.
5. Annuities come in many shapes and sizes. Seek professional advice on what may or may not be appropriate for your situation as well as which companies have solid financial ratings.

Of course, there's more! We've discussed balancing income and spend down. But many more traps await you in preserving and protecting your wealth. From navigating the land mines associated with distributions from your IRAs and qualified plans to the risk of long-term convalescent care to distributing your assets at death.

Chapter V

The Roles of IRAs and Company Retirement Plans

Conversation Over a Beer

While sharing a beer and a Saturday afternoon at the pub, Kevin revealed the plight of his cousin Timothy to his drinking buddy Pat.

"It's a sad thing," he opined. "Poor Timothy worked for forty years for a company with the best pension plan in the whole world. Now he's livin' in the poorhouse. Just two weeks before he was to retire, his company went bankrupt, takin' his pension down with it."

"For sure, 'tis a bad thing," Pat agreed. "What happened to bankrupt them? Tough competition? Corporate shenanigans? Embezzlement? Changing marketplace?"

"No," Kevin replied, "it was none of that."

"Then what was it?" Pat pressed.

"The company couldn't afford the cost of the pension plan."

Rather than defined benefit pension plans such as the one poor "Timothy" had, the majority of Americans today have IRAs or their company retirement plan brethren, 401(k)s. For many people contemplating retirement, they are a significant portion of their assets. Many financial advisors believe that the way you handle your tax-deferred money is the single most important piece of your overall financial plan.

Major concerns regarding the dispositions of your IRA include:

- How and when should you take your distribution from your company retirement plan(s) and other IRA accounts?
- How much should you (or must you) take out at one time or each year?
- Who should you name as beneficiary?
- When you take money out, or inherit an IRA, what are the tax consequences?

If you have significant assets in these tax-deferred IRA and retirement plan accounts, these are among some of the most important and complex financial decisions you will ever make. The answers to these questions will depend on a number of unique personal factors.

When you leave your employer, you will receive a "retirement plan distribution package." It will contain important disclosures and forms relating to your distribution options. It's important that you make the right decisions, and complete these forms properly. Most people approaching retirement do not fully understand the hidden negative consequences of making the wrong choices. You and your heirs could end up paying enormous—and unneeded—taxes and penalties!

Whether you will be receiving tax-deferred money, are the legal representative for, or are the beneficiary of these kinds of accounts, it is extremely important that you seek the services of competent, informed professionals such as a tax advisor, financial advisor, or attorney.

This chapter will discuss the basics of IRAs and company retirement plans, important tax considerations, beneficiary issues, and common mistakes people make with IRAs.

Understanding the Basics

There are two basic types of company retirement plans. Defined benefit plans and defined contribution plans.

Defined Benefit Plans (generally referred to as pension plans)

These plans provide for a monthly payment after you retire, usually based on a formula that takes into account your years of service, and a percentage of an average of the last few years of your income. The assets of such plans are invested by your company on your behalf, usually by a pension board or employee benefits committee appointed by the board of directors of the firm.

When you retire, some defined benefit plans will allow the direct rollover of your entire account balance into an IRA. Other defined benefit plans only allow for a monthly payment. If your defined benefit plan only allows for a monthly payment, you will need to carefully consider which option is best for you.

Defined Contribution Plans (generally referred to as 401(k) plans, profit sharing, SEP, SIMPLE, savings plans, etc.)

These plans allow you and/or your employer to make contributions into your account, usually based on a percentage of your current income. Then you, the employee, make the investment decisions (often among a limited number of choices). What you have at the time of you retirement is dependent on the investment choices you've made while you were a participant and is not based on a monthly formula that the plan promises to pay you as long as you live.

Defined contribution plans usually allow for the direct rollover of your account balance into an IRA.

A number of companies provide both types of plans, though pension plans are being discontinued or are being offered less often, primarily due to the long-term obligation incurred by the plan when employees retire.

A Greater Understanding

Your IRA is different from most other assets in a number of ways. Here are some important rules:

- Interests in an IRA cannot be gifted, but you can certainly *take money out* of an IRA, pay taxes, and gift what is left over (be careful of the annual limits on gifting though, or you could end up paying even more tax).
- If you leave your IRA to a nonspouse, there are a number of rules your heirs need to follow in order to avoid unnecessary taxes (more on this later under the section on beneficiaries).
- Assets in an IRA receive no capital gains treatment. Distributions are subject to ordinary income tax.
- IRAs pass directly to the beneficiary that you name in your IRA document and are not subject to probate. They do not pass through a will. You,

therefore, need to understand the rules that apply to naming beneficiaries, and the issues relating to the term "designated beneficiary."

- Unlike a stock, at your death, your heirs do not receive the value of your account at your death as their new basis for purposes of calculating capital gains—also referred to as "step-up in cost basis."
- IRAs do not qualify for capital-gains tax treatment either during your life, or after your death. In other words, all distributions from your IRA that your heirs receive will be subject to ordinary income tax, paid at their top tax bracket.
- Title cannot be transferred to a trust. The owner of an IRA must be an individual, but you *can* name a trust as beneficiary if it is set up properly.

Required Minimum Distributions

The law demands that IRAs are subject to "minimum distributions," that is, at certain milestones, a portion of the accumulated monies must be paid out, and taxes paid upon these. IRAs are subject to minimum distributions in the following circumstances:

- when you turn seventy and a half (or at the latest no later than April 1 of the year following the year that you turn seventy and a half)
- when you inherit an IRA and properly retitle that IRA by September 30 (October 31 for trusts) of the year following the year that the owner died. (The original owner's required minimum distribution (RMD) must still be taken by December 31 of the year the original account holder died, if they were over seventy and a half.

Taxes

Your IRA may be subject to one or more of the following taxes: income tax, estate tax, state taxes, generation skipping tax, and various penalty taxes. The simple rule you should remember is this:

*Don't Take Out Too Little, Too
Much, Too Early, or Too Late!*

- Too little:
Your distributions should take into account the other taxes you are paying, and you should try to pay the least overall tax possible. This is especially true in the five to ten years leading up to age seventy and a half.

For example if you have a large IRA and are living on current assets and income that does not take you deep into the tax table, then you should consider taking some money out of your IRA now. You will pay a lower tax on those distributions now, instead of the otherwise higher tax you might pay once you reach seventy and a half and are forced to take your minimum distributions.

Also, keep in mind that there is a 50 percent penalty for not taking out your full, required minimum distribution.

- Too much:
Don't be forced to pay unnecessary taxes, which can include federal income taxes, state income taxes, estate and generation skipping taxes either you while you are alive, or by your heirs after you die because you did not name a proper designated beneficiary, or because your heirs don't understand the inherited IRA rules! Distributions should take into account other "already taxed" assets you may have that you may wish to use first to reduce your overall tax.

- Too early:
If you take distributions before age fifty-nine and a half (unless you take your distributions under special rules referred to as "section 72(t)") you will generally pay a 10 percent penalty *in addition to ordinary income taxes.*

The special rules and formulae under which early distribution *can* be made without penalty are complex and necessitate professional advice. If you deviate form the formula you originally choose, you can be required to pay the 10 percent penalty on all of the distributions you have taken up to that point.

- Too late:
As mentioned above, there is a 50 percent penalty for not taking out your full, required minimum distribution. Additionally, if your beneficiary does not properly retitle an inherited IRA by September 30 of the year following the death of the owner and take the required minimum distribution by December 31, the entire balance will have to come out within five years and be needlessly subject to tax.

Special Comment for Very Large IRA: If you leave a very large IRA when you die, you may find that the balance left to your heirs is nearly destroyed by estate taxes, income taxes, and/or generation skipping taxes. In a worst-case scenario, your beneficiaries could lose up to 70 percent of the account balance to these taxes!

One simple way to reduce this overall tax is to "prepay the estate tax at a discount" by taking partial distributions before you die, paying taxes on those distributions, and purchasing a "second to die" life insurance policy which will cover this triple tax when the surviving spouse dies.

There is no income tax or estate tax when the first spouse passes away, assuming that the beneficiary is the surviving spouse, and the surviving spouse transfers the IRA over to his or her own IRA. All of these taxes will come due when the second spouse passes away. If this applies to you, isn't it smarter to share a small portion of your IRA with an insurance company now, in order to avoid sharing up to 70 percent with 280 million strangers (the IRS) later?

Conventional Beneficiaries: Don't Make the IRS the Beneficiary of Your IRA!

What happens to your IRA when you die will depend on who you named as the beneficiary.

When the owner of an individual retirement account dies, one or more *designated beneficiaries* or their legal representatives must choose how to manage the inheritance.

If you are the beneficiary of an IRA, you will need to know the following:

- The original account holder's age at time of death. Which type of IRA is being inherited: traditional or Roth?
- Date the account was opened if a Roth IRA.
- The identity of the beneficiary. Most people usually choose one or more of the following: spouse, children and/or grandchildren, trust, charity(ies), or estate.
- Had the original account holder started taking required minimum distributions?

Usually, the beneficiary is the original account holder's surviving spouse. The choices available to a spouse beneficiary depend on a variety of factors, including whether the original account holder had reached age seventy and a half, and if the spouse was the sole beneficiary.

Generally speaking, if the spouse was the sole beneficiary, and the decedent was over seventy and a half when he or she died, the surviving spouse may

- roll over part or all of the balance into his or her IRA and continue to defer taxes until he or she reaches age seventy and a half, in other words treat the IRA as his or her own and have the right to name new beneficiaries, etc.;
- take a lump-sum distribution and pay taxes on the lump sum taken;
- establish an inherited IRA and take minimum distributions each year; or,
- utilize a combination of the above after splitting the account into separate pieces, treating each piece differently.

Rolling over the entire balance into his or her IRA might not always be the best option for a surviving spouse. For example; if your spouse is under fifty-nine and a half, and will need money from the IRA, he or she may be subject to early withdrawal penalties.

If the original account holder was less than seventy and a half, similar rules apply with the following exceptions:

- The surviving spouse may roll over part or all of the balance into his or her IRA and continue to defer taxes until he or she reaches age seventy and a half—in other words treat the IRA as his or her own.
- The surviving spouse may take a lump-sum distribution and pay taxes on the lump sum taken.
- You may establish an inherited IRA and take minimum distributions each year. This distribution is based on the surviving spouse's life expectancy (ordinary taxes must be paid, but no 10 percent penalty applies even if the surviving spouse is under fifty-nine and a half). The distribution must start in the year after the original account holder died, or start in the year the original account holder would have reached seventy and a half, whichever is later.
- You may establish an inherited IRA and take the entire balance out by the end of the fifth year after the original account holder died.
- Another option is a combination of the above after splitting into separate pieces and treating each piece differently, according to the rules that apply to that piece.

Nonspouse as Beneficiary

The choices available to a nonspouse beneficiary depend on a variety of factors, including whether the original account holder reached age seventy and a half, and if there were multiple beneficiaries. If there are multiple beneficiaries, it is usually best to split the IRA into separate pieces and establish a separate, "inherited IRA" for each beneficiary. If the inherited IRA is not set up this way, then the oldest beneficiary's life expectancy (translates to quicker, larger distributions) must be used to determine annual distributions.

Generally speaking, in the event that a nonspouse is the beneficiary and the decedent was under seventy and a half, there are various choices for the beneficiary. He or she

- may take a lump-sum distribution;
- must take out the entire balance by December 31 of the fifth year following the original account holder's death; and
- if eligible, may elect to establish an inherited IRA, which will allow the nonspouse beneficiary(ies) to take out the distributions from the inherited IRA by December 31 of the year after the original account holder's death. Distributions are based on the beneficiary's life expectancy reduced by one each year.

A nonspouse beneficiary cannot roll over the amount into his or her own IRA! Additional rules and exclusions apply that should be discussed with your professional advisor.

When establishing an inherited IRA, it is important to understand that the IRA account must be retitled by September 30 of the year following the year the IRA owner died. It must be retitled as follows: "John Doe, deceased (or decedent), IRA FBO Steve Jones." It is important that both the decedent's name *and* the name of the beneficiary both appear in the title of the inherited IRA. Beneficiaries pay income taxes as they receive distributions, but they are only required to take out a certain *minimum* amount of money each year and are, therefore, still able to defer the remaining funds in much the same way as the original account holder. By utilizing an inherited IRA in this fashion—only withdrawing the minimum amount each year and leaving the rest to grow—the additional money available to a beneficiary over time is remarkable. The following table illustrates this point:

Your Inherited IRA—What Is It Really Worth?

Total IRA Distributions from Inherited IRA over Beneficiaries Lifetime*

Age	Life Expectancy	$ 100,000	$ 500,000	$ 1,000,000
25	58.2	$ 5,271,719	$ 26,358,598	$ 52,717,197
35	48.5	$ 2,702,037	$ 13,510,185	$ 27,020,371
45	38.8	$ 1,240,721	$ 6,203,609	$ 12,407,218
55	29.6	$ 659,844	$ 3,299,222	$ 6,598,444

*   Assumptions: only required minimum distributions withdrawn, 10 percent annual return. Distribution subject to income taxes.

Note: The authors grant that a sustained, thirty-year, 10 percent annual return is an unreasonable expectation for most portfolios but is used here to make a dramatic point: Handled properly, a large inherited IRA can provide a substantial income stream for two generations—even if the rate of return is much lower.

Trust as Beneficiary

The choices available to a trust as a beneficiary depends on whether a trust's beneficiaries may be taken into account, as well as other factors, such as whether the account holder had reached his or her RBD. In order for a trust's beneficiaries to be taken into account in determining the choices, the trust must meet each of these requirements:

- Is the trust irrevocable (or did it become irrevocable when the account holder died)?
- Is the trust valid under state law?
- Does the trust name identifiable beneficiaries?
- Does the custodian possess a copy of the trust agreement (or a list of all beneficiaries of the trust, certified by the trustee as a complete list of beneficiaries)?

Estate as Beneficiary

This is the most onerous of all forms of beneficiary and gives the beneficiaries of the decedent's estate these options:

If the account holder was *under* seventy and a half:

- lump-sum distribution; or,
- inherited IRA (beneficiary must take the entire balance out by the end of the fifth year after the year that the original account holder died).

If the account holder was *over* seventy and a half:

- lump-sum distribution;
- or, inherited IRA (life expectancy based on the single life expectancy of the original account holder).

Special Note: If a charity is the beneficiary of an IRA outright, then the same distribution rules apply as outlined in estate as beneficiary above, except that the charity will pay no tax on money received, nor will the estate have to pay tax on the funds distributed. So when this is the case, the charity usually takes the entire balance when it becomes available.

The foregoing only scratches the surface of the rules for IRAs, yet another reason why the advice of a professional advisor isn't a luxury—it's a necessity.

Special Rules for Roth IRAs

The rules that apply to Roth IRA distributions, though similar, have crucial differences. Some of the important differences:

- *Five-year holding period:* Roth IRA distributions consist of after-tax contributions and earnings. Contribution amounts are always distributed tax free, but a five-year holding period applies to earnings. If the account has been opened for at least five years at the time of the account holder's death, earnings are distributed tax free and penalty free. If earnings are distributed before the account has been opened for five years, the earnings are taxable, but penalty free. If not, earnings stay in the account and are taxed until the account is five years old. Early withdrawals are subject to all applicable tax, including possible early withdrawal penalties and withholding requirements. There are various rules that apply to a spouse, nonspouse, and trust beneficiary.
- *Roth IRAs are not subject to required minimum distributions* during an account holder's lifetime. However, after the account holder's death, in order for these distributions of earnings to be tax free, the account must be opened for at least five years. (Other rules apply depending upon who inherits the account).
- *If the account was open less than five years* at the time of the original account holder's death, any earnings withdrawn will be taxed, until the account is five years old. In addition, if a spouse beneficiary chooses to treat the Roth IRA as his or her own, the spouse beneficiary usually must also wait until age fifty-nine and a half to take distributions tax free.

Roth IRA Beneficiaries

The options available to beneficiaries of a Roth IRA are dependent on the identity of the beneficiary: spouse, nonspouse, trust or estate, and some other considerations. Before you decide which choice is best for you, you should consult with your tax advisor to evaluate the impact it will have.

Common Mistakes:

Now that we have covered the basic rules, here are some of the most common mistakes, divided into five areas:

While you are accumulating:

Mistake 1: Not participating in your company retirement plans to the maximum extent allowed, or not participating at all. Your company retirement plan is one of the best places for you to accumulate wealth over the long term, especially when you take into consideration that none of your contributions are taxed, for perhaps twenty, thirty, or forty years; most employers offer a matching provision for a portion of your contributions, and maximum allowable contributions generally increase every year. It is simply unwise not to take advantage of this company benefit, but don't stop at the company match. All of your employee contributions come right off the top of your income and are not reported as earned income. Uncle Sam has given us an incentive to put away as much as possible.

Mistake 2: Putting too much of your money in your company's stock (too risky). A widely accepted general rule of thumb is never to have more than 15 percent of your wealth invested in any one individual stock. The risk that you incur is higher than a well-diversified portfolio and is beyond the acceptable risk tolerance of most individuals (whether they really understand that or not!). When you see your account balance approaching 15 percent in one stock, it is a good idea to rebalance your portfolio to a more suitable, diversified investment mix tied to your goals, time horizon, and overall risk tolerance. Highly paid executives have other special political considerations that need to be taken into account when implementing this rule, but the rule is a sound and prudent one nonetheless.

Mistake 3: Putting too much of your money into a money-market account or guaranteed account (too conservative). Retirement plan participants generally have too much of their money invested in the most conservative investment options. Given the experience many people had during 2000 to 2002, this is understandable, but putting all of your money into the most conservative option can be a mistake, just like putting too much of your money in the most risky options! A better approach would be to assess your risk tolerance, develop your allocation from among different asset classes, then periodically rebalance. Keep in mind that the long-term (fifty-year) return of equities is approximately 11 percent, and the long-term return of bonds has been approximately 5 percent. The closer you are to retirement, the more conservative you ought to be, conservative being a relative term defined by you in collaboration with your advisor.

Mistake 4: Trading your account excessively. It is seductive to believe that you can "beat the market." Most people, including many well-regarded money managers, don't. Your best approach may be to periodically review your allocations and rebalance just a few times a year.

Special Note: Some companies will allow you to receive a lump-sum distribution or will allow you to directly roll over some or all of your account balance after age fifty-nine and a half, even if you're still employed. This is typically called an "in-service distribution." Is this right for you? That is a subjective question with many other factors to consider including your age, certain guarantees that may be offered by your current plan, and your desire to exercise more control over your investment choices.

When you retire:

Mistake 5: Not planning ahead.

Waiting just prior to your retirement date to understand your distribution options can be devastating. When you retire, you will generally have the following four options:

- Roll the money over into an IRA.
- Leave your money in the plan.
- Take a lump-sum distribution.
- Transfer the money into your new employer's plan.

Generally speaking, if you have an opportunity to roll over your retirement plan balance into an IRA, the advantages outweigh the disadvantages. However, you will need to understand both sides of this question to make the decision that's right for you. There will always be some individuals for whom an IRA rollover is not appropriate (if for example, you are between fifty-five and fifty-nine and a half and will need some of your tax-deferred funds to live on). Some people feel that if you are able to receive a distribution, leaving your money in your company retirement plan could be a big mistake because the rules associated with company retirement plans are generally more restrictive than IRA rules, both for you and especially for your beneficiaries, and you will have fewer investment options.

Unless you plan on spending your entire balance right away, it is generally not a good idea to take a lump sum and pay all of the taxes all at once. For most people, this is often the worst alternative.

If you plan on working after retirement and becoming employed by a firm with a defined contribution retirement plan, you are allowed to transfer your current plan balance into your new employer's plan. Even though current rules allow you to roll over your balance into a new employer's retirement plan, you are generally better off rolling that money into an IRA for the same reasons mentioned above.

Your concern will now generally shift to income *planning.*

You will want to structure your affairs to ensure that your money lasts longer than you do! This generally means a more conservative approach than when you were in an accumulation mode. You should clearly understand your distribution options at least a few months before you need to send in your paperwork to request your retirement distribution. This will give you some time to think through the most appropriate choices for you. Making last-minute decisions about something this important can be dangerous! Once you send the paperwork in, your choices are usually final and cannot be changed.

Some things you will want to consider:

First, your company retirement plan usually only offers you limited investment choices, if you roll those funds into what is called a "self-directed IRA," you are in control of where those assets are invested. With proper guidance, you can make wise investment choices that provide more diversification, and that may be more suitable for your risk tolerance and income needs.

Second, and probably more important, if you have named nonspouse beneficiaries, they will most likely be forced to take the entire balance out all in one year (or perhaps over five years depending on your plan's rules). This would force them to pay taxes on the entire balance over that time instead of taking much smaller distributions over say a thirty—or forty-year time horizon. The difference in total dollars paid out can be huge. "What's the difference?" you might be thinking. "I'll be gone anyway." Well, why not structure your affairs to share your wealth with the people you love or causes you care about, rather than with the IRS?

What Should I Do with Company Stock in My Company Retirement Plan?

Serious mistakes are often made when rolling over stock shares. First, remember the 15-percent rule. If you have shares of stock in a company retirement plan that represent more than 15 percent of your net worth, prudence would suggest that you should diversify, no matter how good you think the company is! Remember the "Nifty Fifty" stocks of the early '70s? A number of those companies are no longer around!

Stock in a company retirement plan requires special consideration. First, if you have "low basis" in your stock, you may want to take a distribution of that stock and then sell it. You will pay ordinary income tax on the basis, but only pay capital-gains tax on the net unrealized appreciation (special rules apply). If you roll the stock over into an IRA, there will be no income tax when you sell it in the IRA, but you will pay ordinary income tax on any distributions that you take out later.

If you receive stock certificates as part of a lump-sum distribution, you will need to be especially careful. If you decide to roll over your stock, make sure beforehand that your IRA custodian will accept the stock. Some IRA custodians will not accept stock certificates! For example, many banks and credit unions only allow investing in CDs or a money-market fund and don't offer the option of a true, self-directed IRA. Also, many investment companies offer you a choice of investments, but only in their own mutual funds. You should look for an IRA that allows proper diversification.

Having Too Many IRA Custodians

It is crucial to understand the difference between what your IRA custodian allows and what the IRS allows. You must comply with whichever set of rules is more restrictive!

As tax laws have changed over the years, some custodians (this applies to all types of custodians including banks, brokerage firms, credit unions, insurance companies, etc.) have not kept up with these revisions and have not changed their documents to allow what the IRS allows—for example, allowing the establishment of an inherited IRA.

You may, therefore, find yourself in a situation where the IRS will allow one thing, but your custodian requires you or your heirs to do something different— oftentimes more restrictive. The same comment applies to company retirement plans (for example, nonspouse beneficiaries are often required to take all of the money out within one year and pay tax on the entire balance).

Roll over pretax, after-tax portions:

Under the new tax laws that became effective January 1, 2002, after-tax contributions are now also eligible to be rolled over! If you roll over or transfer any part of these after-tax contributions, then there will not be a penalty for rolling over too much! But keep in mind that you will need to keep track of the "already taxed" amount that you rolled over each year on your tax return by filing a form 8606.

When you reach age seventy and a half:

Be sure you understand the required minimum-distribution rules and how they apply to you! If you don't take out the proper RMD amount, you will end up paying up to 50 percent of the amount you didn't take out as a tax penalty.

Special Note: You may take distributions for all or any combination of your IRAs in order to meet your RMD. A good idea is just to have one IRA that will allow you to diversify your holdings inside of that account so as to keep your calculations simple and avoid mistakes.

Before you die:

Make sure you have properly named your beneficiary!

It is *never* a good idea to name your estate the beneficiary of your IRA. This will impose the most restrictive rules on those who will inherit your IRA. If you name a trust, it is a good idea to consider language that will easily allow the different beneficiaries to split their interests in the trusts into separate inherited IRAs, so as not to be forced to take money out based on the oldest, or most restrictive, beneficiary.

Make sure you consider the combination of all possible taxes that may be imposed on your IRA.

These include federal and state income taxes, along with estate taxes and possibly generation skipping tax as discussed earlier.

When you inherit an IRA:

You cannot roll over an IRA into your own IRA unless you are the decedent's spouse!

If you do, you may be subject to a 50 percent overfunding tax penalty!

If you have the choice, you are probably better off taking distributions over your lifetime versus the five-year option.

The worst option is taking the money out all at once and paying 35 percent or more in federal income taxes!

You must use the correct language when establishing an inherited IRA.

Remember the IRA must be properly retitled by September 30 of the year following the year the IRA owner died as follows: "John Doe, deceased (or decedent), IRA FBO Steve Jones." It is important that both the decedent's name appears, *and* the name of the beneficiary also appears in the title of the inherited IRA. Beneficiaries pay income taxes as they receive distributions, but they are only required to take out a certain *minimum* amount of money and are, therefore, still able to defer the remaining funds in the same way as the original account holder did.

Be extra careful when naming a trust as beneficiary.

You must comply with the rules in order for the trust to be considered a "designated beneficiary."

Be sure that you properly calculate your inherited IRA RMD.

If you take out too little, you will be subject to penalties and more taxes.

The rules affecting IRAs are constantly changing. Misinterpretation of newly changed rules or continued application of obsolete rules can have a large and potentially devastating impact upon your personal finances and those of your descendants.

Appropriate, regular, ongoing professional advice is essential to achievement of your goals.

Chapter VI

Protecting Yourself in Retirement:

The Potential Devastation of Long-Term Health Care

Not a myth, but a very quotable quote:

If I had known I was going to live so long, I would have taken better care of myself.

—George Burns

Long-term health care insurance is not simply needed for an unfortunate possibility; it is *likely* that long-term care will be required, and it *will* be devastating if not planned for properly.

The financial demands of care for older individuals with functional limitations, (often due to unexpected diseases such as Alzheimer's, Parkinson's, multiple sclerosis, or the unfortunate result of an auto, sporting, or farming accident, or other chronic disabling condition due to the natural process of aging) could dramatically accelerate the depletion of your retirement nest egg.

In addition to the financial burden, there is a significant emotional and physical burden imposed on the caretaker. We all know someone who has spent years caring for an ailing parent or loved one, often while still responsible for raising their own children. There is little time or energy left for much else in the caretaker's own life.

"Long-term health care," as generally defined in terms of insurance, is care needed by those suffering from chronic physical or mental impairment which lasts at least ninety days. Insurance benefits are triggered when you are unable to perform two out of six activities of daily living (bathing, dressing, transferring, feeding, toileting, and incontinence), or in the event of cognitive impairments such as Alzheimer's disease or dementia.

According to the Health Insurance Association of America, approximately 50 percent of all Americans will need long-term health care at some point during their lives.

Long Term Health Care—
The Cost of *Not* Including It in Your Retirement Planning

No matter how you've earned, saved, and invested, there is one pitfall that can quickly destroy your retirement plans: the need for long-term care for you or a loved one.

Most of us fail to consider the impact long-term care expenses will have on our retirement incomes. Even abbreviated long-term care can quickly decimate a nest egg. The consequences of extended long-term care can be catastrophic. Extended health care costs—beyond what are covered by private and government programs—are one of the major causes of personal bankruptcies in the United States.

The costs of such care can rapidly deplete most individuals' retirement portfolios, leaving the stay-at-home partner with an empty nest egg. Consider the impact of long-term care costs on a retirement portfolio. Starting with a $500,000 retirement nest egg and no debt, at current prices, that entire nest egg would be gone within just six years, if either member of the couple required long-term care!

$500,000 Nest Egg Example						
Onset of long long-term care expenses	Year 1	Year 2	Year 3	Year 4	Year 5	Year 6
Invested Assets	$ 500,000	$ 435,000	$ 360,900	$ 276,867	$ 182,002	$ 75,335
Annual yield	$ 30,000	$ 26,100	$ 21,654	$ 16,612	$ 10,920	$ 4,520
Household living expenses of healthy spouse	$ 50,000	$ 52,500	$ 55,125	$ 57,881	$ 60,775	$ 63,814
Nursing home expenses	$ 45,000	$ 47,700	$ 50,562	$ 53,596	$ 56,811	$ 60,220
Capital remaining	$ 435,000	$ 360,900	$ 276,867	$ 182,002	$ 75,335	BROKE!

This chart shows how quickly a family's nest egg of $500,000 (savings, investments, or retirement funds) would be depleted, assuming household living expenses are $50,000 per year (plus 5 percent annual inflation), the cost of long-term care expenses, assuming *nursing home stay of $45,000 (plus 6 percent annual medical inflation rate), and the remaining capital earning 6 percent per year, paid at the beginning of the year.*

The assumptions used are only for illustrative purposes. Geographic locations, return on investments, individual circumstances, and medical and financial inflation rates will impact these results accordingly.

As you can see by the above illustration, at the end of six years, the couple would be broke utilizing only $45,000 per year for nursing-home costs adjusted for inflation.

But these costs are escalating far more *rapidly* than inflation. According to a survey conducted by Genworth Financial Inc.'s long-term care insurance group, the average annual cost of a private room in a nursing home was $65,200 in 2004—a 13 percent increase over the average amount in 2003.

The Medicare Fallacy

Many persons facing retirement mistakenly assume that Medicare will pay for long-term health care costs; nothing could be further from the truth. Like many Americans, the couple in the above "$500,000 nest egg" example assumed that long-term health care expenses—just like other types of health care expenses— would be covered by Medicare after retirement.

Limitations and restrictions in Medicare eligibility are such that very few, if any, long-term health care services are covered. Medicare was designed for short-term acute care, and short-term rehabilitative stays in a rehabilitation center or long-term care facility as outlined in the following chart.

Medicare Pays for Skilled Care Only (Following Three-Day Hospitalization)

Benefit	Medicare Pays
First 20 days of skilled care services	100% coverage
Next 80 days, *your daily copay*	100% after *$114.00** per day Total out-of-pocket cost to you is *$9,120*
After 100 days	Medicare offers *no benefits* at this point and you are responsible for 100% of the expenses!

*This amount is adjusted each year. *Source: www.medicare.gov*

Even if you did receive benefits from Medicare, how will you pay for long-term health care costs after one hundred days?

Chronic diseases such as Alzheimer's, Parkinson's, or multiple sclerosis require custodial care, which is not covered by Medicare.

Custodial care is personal care, to help you meet personal needs such as bathing, dressing, eating, and transferring from the bed to a chair, and toileting. This type of care can be administered in your own home, around-the-clock, in an assisted living facility, adult day-care center, or in a nursing home. Please note, however, that each type of care has various costs associated with it.

Most people would rather receive care in their home as long as possible. At a current cost of approximately $18.75 per hour, it would add up to $450 per day for 24/7 coverage or $164,250 per year. In twenty years, using 5 percent inflation factor, this amount grows to a staggering $709,560 per year. Even the strongest retirement portfolio will suffer under the weight of these costs unless steps are taken beforehand to help mitigate some of these expenses.

For these reasons, the purchase of long-term health care insurance is an essential element of most Americans' retirement portfolio planning. The cost and likelihood of unavailability of such coverage increases dramatically as people age.

For most persons, planning their retirement portfolios, the purchase of long-term health care insurance—the sooner the better—is highly advisable.

Insurance is *essential* to eliminating or mitigating the consequences of long-term health care costs.

Long-term care is not just nursing home assistance. It includes settings such as

- Your own home
- Assisted living facility
- Adult day-care facility
- Hospice care
- Nursing home

Most Americans' have their heads in the sand. However, their assets are exposed to the long-term care crisis.

Every day the media is alive with items about the aging of America, the overburdened state of Social Security, the health care cost explosion, and other equally depressing, related stories. Yet even though we may feel we've done a great job of accumulating enough wealth to see us through our twilight years, we embrace the ostrich syndrome when confronting the likelihood of long-term care, putting our heads in the sand, and leaving our assets exposed.

Very few Americans can afford to do this without impacting their retirement portfolio. The sooner we accept the likelihood of long-term health care costs depleting our assets, the more affordably we can deal with it.

Why it is important to purchase now, versus waiting? Not only will it cost more if you wait, changes in your health could impact your ability to even *purchase* a plan.

The Cost of Waiting

Currently, purchasing a long-term care-insurance plan at age sixty-five would cost $62,640 over twenty years. As the following table shows, had you purchased it at age fifty-five, you would have only paid $28,800. This represents a 46 percent increase in the cost of premiums just for waiting ten years.

Lifetime Premium Payment Purchased at <u>Age 55</u>

Policy Period	Age	Total Premium Paid	Policy Paid in Full
First Year	55	$ 1,440	No
After 10 Years	65	$ 14,400	No
After 20 Years	75	$ 28,800	No

Lifetime Premium Payment Purchased at <u>Age 65</u>

Policy Period	Age	Total Premium Paid	Policy Paid in Full
First Year	65	$ 3,132	No
After 10 Years	75	$ 31,320	No
After 20 Years	85	$ 62,640	No

Monthly Benefit: $3,000 (or $100 per day)
Benefit Period: Lifetime
Elimination Period   30 days
(Deductible)
Inflation Option   5% Compound per year

This is a sampling of one particular plan design (Genworth Financial's flagship policy—privileged choice). There are a variety of plan designs available in the marketplace today to fit the budget of every person that considers this program. These include longer elimination periods, (60 days, 90 days, and 180 days) shorter benefit periods (from two years to twenty years), and the daily benefit can be adjusted to reflect the cost of care in the local retirement community. One new and interesting plan design several carriers have introduced is called "shared care." Under this plan, one policy is issued for a couple which allows that couple to share in the same "pool of money."

Consideration of your plan design needs to take into account what state you retire in, as costs vary by state and region. Further, even within individual states or regions, cost can vary depending upon specific locales. The following chart compares current average daily long-term care costs by region and state.

LTC Cost Averages

2003 National Avg.= **$158 day**

$57,700 year

$232

Source: GE's 2003 LTCI Nursing Home Survey
Skilled or Intermediate Care Facilities

Daily Projections:
2006=**$181**
2008=**$198**
2010=**$217**
2020=**$340**

Pay Now or Pay Later

Long-term health care costs are more than a financial issue. It's really a family issue that every family should address. When the unexpected happens to you and your family, will you be prepared? Long-term health insurance planning provides a safety net to protect you, your family, and your retirement dreams and goals. It is a plan to be included in every retirement planning strategy. It affords you the freedom to make choices that fit your health care needs. Don't leave your retirement-planning strategies exposed to this crisis as you reach retirement.

Planning ahead for long-term health care expenses has never been more important than it is today.

Chapter VII

Estate Planning

A Thought on Passing
(As Opposed to a Passing Thought)

There was a look of surprised grief on the faces of Horace's children and their families.

As his attorney explained the status of the departed Horace's estate to them, they realized the familiar old saying that they had heard all their lives was untrue.

Instead of the long-winded reading of the will they had expected, the attorney's words—all five of them—were direct and to the point: "He took it with him."

A ship without a planned route is unlikely to make its port. Just as you need planned goals for your investment and retirement strategies, you need professionally advised planning to ensure the estate you leave behind ends up where you desire.

To plan, however, requires a basic legal understanding of the types of property ownership and various means of transferring this ownership to the ones you leave behind.

Property Ownership

There are three basic ways to own property: sole ownership, joint ownership, and trust ownership. Within these three categories, there are additional choices.

Sole Ownership

In sole ownership, property is owned in the name of an individual and can only be used, transferred, or disposed of by the owner alone or by the owner's agent during his or her lifetime.

At death, the powers given to an agent cease. After death, property in an owner's name alone can only be accessed, used, transferred, or disposed of with "letters of office" issued by the circuit court of the county in which the property owner lived. Property held in sole ownership becomes "probate property," meaning ownership can only be transferred using probate court proceedings. In some cases, probate proceedings can be avoided by using a Small Estate Affidavit.

Tenants in common, joint tenancy, and *tenants by the entirety* are all forms of *joint ownership*, each with its own peculiarities.

1) *Tenants in Common*
   Owning property as tenants in common means that each owner has an undivided, fractional interest in the property. The same rules apply which apply to sole ownership apply to the interest of each tenant in common. For illustration, Charlene and Bill could own 40 percent and 60 percent (respectively) of a piece of property. If Bill passed away, his 60 percent interest in the property would be treated in the same way as if it was "sole ownership": not a happy situation for Charlene who now finds 60 percent of the property, in which she has an interest, tied up in probate.

2) *Joint Tenancy*
   Joint tenants are owners of an undivided interest in property. In other words, they share equal control over the same piece of property. In terms of the estate, though, there is an added benefit to this type of ownership: the surviving joint tenant automatically becomes the owner of the deceased joint tenant's interest. No probate is required.

   Joint tenancies can pose problems, however. For example, elderly people might name an adult child as a joint tenant on bank accounts to facilitate bill paying during their waning years. The problem with this use of joint tenancy arises if the elderly person never intended to make a gift of that account and assumed that the joint tenant would divide the account among siblings after death.

   In most states, the courts would assume that the surviving joint tenant is now the owner of the account.

Tenants by the Entirety

Tenants by the entirety is a form of joint tenancy for married couples and, in most states, is only available for ownership of the married couple's primary residence.

The added feature of tenancy by the entirety is that a creditor of one spouse can not attach or lien the marital home in the event a judgment is obtained against only one spouse. This is a very useful type of joint tenancy used for asset protection if one or both spouses have creditor issues or are in a profession with personal liability exposure.

Trust Ownership

A trust is a form of ownership in which the legal owner of the property (the trustee) holds the property for the benefit of someone else (the beneficiary). Trusts can be revocable or irrevocable.

Revocable trusts are trusts which can be amended or restated or revoked at any time. They are *not* asset protection trusts and will be included in the grantor's estate for estate tax purposes. Some revocable trusts are very limited and hold a single piece of property or asset. Examples of these types of trusts are Totten trusts (often called "payable on death accounts") and land trusts. Other revocable trusts known as "living trusts" are more complex trust and can hold multiple types of property.

Advantages of trust ownership can include a reduction in estate taxes and a more seamless transfer of ownership to your successors, with minimal legal entanglement. In case of a known illness, a trust offers an additional benefit: the disability language can be crafted to the needs of the individual and his or her medical problem. With a trust, the successor trustee can quickly access trust accounts to pay medical and funeral expenses and otherwise deal with trust assets.

In a trust, the trustee is the party with centralized control of the assets. If a trust has more than one beneficiary, the trustee is allowed to handle the financial affairs of the grantor before distribution of property and with minimal interference from beneficiaries. Unlike joint tenancies or payable on death accounts, beneficiaries must wait until the trustee pays all medical and funeral expenses, files all necessary tax returns, and pays all taxes. Then the trustee distributes the assets in accordance with the terms of the trust.

Each trust can be designed for the client and family for which it is intended and gives the family much more control in dealing with specific family situations than any other type of ownership.

Trusts have the following advantages over other forms of ownership:

- Trusts provide for management of financial affairs during lifetime disability.
- The determination of disability is handled privately without court supervision.
- Trusts give the trustee the authority to pay just debts and expenses of the estate before distribution of property.
- Trusts allow for creation of subtrusts for beneficiaries to "hold back" assets until prescribed ages or deal with special needs and situations of families.
- Trusts give a full step up in basis for all assets held in trust.

ILLUSTRATION #2

COMPARISON OF PROPERTY OWNERSHIP

	Sole Ownership	Tenants in Common	Joint Tenancy	Tenancy By The Entirety	Totten Trusts	Land Trusts	Joint Living Trusts	Separate Living Trusts
Control During Lifetime	Yes	Yes	Yes	Yes	Yes	Yes	Yes	Yes
Disability Feature	No	No	Limited	Limited	No	No	Yes	Yes
Asset Protection During Lifetime for Owner	No	No	No	Yes	No	No	No	No
Asset Protection for Beneficiary After Death	No	No	No	No	No	No	Yes	Yes
Contain Estate Tax Planning - Use of Exclusion Amount	No	No	No	No	No	No	No	Yes
Mechanism for Payment and Apportionment of Taxes and Expenses Among Heirs / Beneficiaries After Death	No	No	No	No	No	No	Yes	Yes
Directs Disposition After Death	No	No	Yes	Yes	Yes	Yes	Yes	Yes

Types of Trusts

Totten Trusts

Totten trusts are trusts established at banking institutions for a bank account or certificate of deposit. The bank provides the form trust agreement. You cannot make any changes or modifications to the agreement other than to change the beneficiary.

The person opening the account (the "grantor") is usually the trustee and beneficiary of the trust during the grantor's lifetime. Then the trust agreement names beneficiaries who will be entitled to the balance of the account after the death of the grantor. People are attracted to this type of trust because of its simplicity.

However, with this simplicity come limitations. First, unless a power of attorney is clearly defined for the account, an agent will have no power to access the account. Should the grantor become disabled, the account could only be accessed by a court-appointed trustee. Since most people establish these accounts on their own without the advice of legal counsel, the accounts are rarely described in powers of attorney. In the absence of a specific reference in a power of attorney, the only way to access these accounts upon disability is to open a guardianship estate in court. Therefore, they might be inaccessible in the event of a lifetime disability.

Second, these trusts do not provide for the payment of expenses or taxes after death. The beneficiaries can literally "run to the bank" and withdraw the funds. It is left to the executor of the estate or family members who paid for medical bills, funeral expenses, and taxes to seek reimbursement from the beneficiaries.

Payable on death accounts such as Totten trusts can cause many problems that were not foreseen by the owners and rarely provide the "simple" results the owners anticipated.

Land Trusts

Land trusts are matters of state statute and are very popular in states such as Illinois. A bank with "land trust authority" acts as the trustee. The grantor of the land trust is the lifetime beneficiary and can name beneficiaries at death. The land trust only controls the real property within it. Like the Totten trusts, there is usually no provision for lifetime disability.

Other than the fact that it specifically covers only real property, the benefit that distinguishes a land trust from a Totten trust is the "power of direction": a land trust includes the power to sell, convey, or encumber the trust property. It is possible to craft a very specific beneficiary designation and power of direction designation in a land trust, which can be used as a "will or trust substitute." An attorney who specializes in estate planning should do such drafting.

While a land trust is not a proper substitute for a living trust, in some cases in which a home is a person's only major asset, a land trust can act as an effective trust to dispose of it.

A common misconception among property owners is that land trusts afford asset protection for the beneficiaries. This is not true. If, for instance, a lawsuit was brought against the estate, it would be the beneficiaries' responsibility. Nevertheless, land trusts remain popular with owners of rental property. They give the owners anonymity since the owner of record is the bank trustee. Identification of the beneficiaries is only possible through court order.

Living Trusts

Living trusts are more complex trusts which provide for lifetime disability and disposition of property upon death.

Living trusts can hold any kind of property. Most estate planners would recommend that a person establishing a living trust transfer all of his or her nonretirement assets to the trust. In some cases, retirement assets are also transferred to a trust.

Living trusts are the most flexible estate-planning vehicles with which to hold property. Each living trust can be carefully drafted to fit the needs of the person establishing the trust, otherwise known as the "grantor." As soon as the trust is executed, it is effective. It can be freely amended, restated, and revoked during the grantor's lifetime. It can provide for management of assets in the event of disability. At death, it can help achieve estate tax goals and dispose of the grantor's property as he or she desired. If proper planning is done, a living trust can avoid both an expensive guardianship during lifetime and probate proceedings at death.

During the grantor's lifetime, a living trust is merely a way to title property. The grantor keeps complete control over the trust assets. The grantor is both the trustee and the beneficiary of the trust. Accounts titled in a living trust use the grantor's Social Security number as the tax identification number. All interest, dividends, and capital gain from such accounts are reported on the grantor's personal income tax returns. It is not until death that the trust will become a separate taxpayer. A living trust is revocable in that it can be amended or revoked at any time until the grantor's death or permanent disability, whichever occurs first. At that time, it becomes irrevocable.

Usually it is not until permanent disability or death that the successor trustee steps into the shoes of the grantor to act as trustee. The mechanism to become successor trustee is private and simple; usually, the trust document designs a system wherein the trustee automatically becomes successor trustee (1) upon written determination of disability, or (2) upon death. Determination of disability is normally made in writing by the grantor's physician and a family member chosen by the grantor.

Separate Living Trusts

If a married couple's estate is large enough to be taxable, each person should have a separate living trust. Within that trust, there will be a formula tied to the current tax law in the year of death to fully use the applicable exclusion amount, thereby, minimizing the estate taxes of both husband and wife.

Joint Trusts

Joint trusts are trusts in which a married couple holds all of their property jointly within the trust. With joint trusts, clients can enjoy all of the advantages of owning property in trust, while keeping their planning as simple as possible.

After the death of the first spouse, the surviving spouse can continue to enjoy control over the assets. The survivor can withdraw assets at any time and can usually modify or revoke the trust at any time.

The property within the trust is deemed to be marital property in common law states. The disadvantage of joint trusts in common law states is that they result in higher estate taxes. Therefore, if a married couple in a common law state has assets in excess of the applicable exclusion amount, a joint trust is not advised.

Furthermore, joint trusts should not be used if either spouse has nonmarital property, such as an inheritance. If such nonmarital property is added to a joint trust, it will lose its character as nonmarital property.

Where There's a Will, There's a Way: Why You Need One

Every estate plan needs a will *even* if the plan includes a trust. A will controls any property owned in a person's name by that person at the time of death. If a person dies with assets in his or her name alone (as apposed to joint tenancy or trust), the property is "frozen." It cannot be accessed or used without the appointment of an executor.

Even though a will *nominates* an executor, an executor is not *appointed* until the court orders it. Every state has a probate code which will require assets individually owned to be "probated" if their total value exceeds the state limit. Some states have a probate limit as low as $10,000. Others have limits varying from $10,000 to $100,000.

If the total assets in the decedent's name are less than the probate limit, the executor can avoid probate proceedings and transfer the assets of the decedent to the beneficiaries of the will, by use of a small estate affidavit. If the total assets equal or exceed the probate limit, the executor must petition the court for "letters of office" in order to transfer or deal with assets.

The probate process is simply a procedure to transfer assets after death, in an orderly way, to protect the beneficiaries, heirs, and any creditors of the estate. If probate is needed, notices must be sent to all heirs at law and all known creditors, as well as to the beneficiaries named in the will. Therefore, in cases when a person decides to name charities or people other than their "heirs at law," they may want to consider establishing a trust to avoid the notice to heirs. It often puts an executor in a difficult position to send notices of probate to the heirs of a decedent when those heirs will receive nothing under the will (unless it is contested and proven to be invalid).

Even with a trust, an estate plan needs a "pour-over will" which simply states that in the event a person dies with property in that person's own name, such property shall be added to or "poured into" the trust created during life. Even those clients who have transferred most of their assets to trust will often have one bank account, such as a checking account, in that person's own name. The will transfers such assets to the trust. Also, if the decedent was involved in a lawsuit, or if a lawsuit arose as a result of the death (such as a wrongful death action), a probate estate would be needed to continue or commence that lawsuit.

Finally, wills are needed if a person inherited money shortly before death but had not yet received the inheritance. An executor would need to be appointed to take possession of that inheritance.

If you have minor children, you must nominate the guardians of such minor children in a will. Even though you make a will, if minor children lose both of their parents, they become temporary wards of the state until the guardians have been appointed by a court of law. In most cases, the courts will honor the wishes of the parents and appoint the guardians nominated by the parents in the will.

Powers of Attorney for Health Care and Property and Living Will

In addition to a will and trust, a complete estate plan will always include powers of attorney for health care and property, *as well* as a living will. These documents are governed by state statute and vary from state to state.

Generally, a health care power of attorney or health care directive permits a person to appoint agents to make health care decisions for that person in the event of a disability. Health care decisions covered by the power of attorney can range from the use of medications, surgery elections, and the withdrawal of life-sustaining procedures. With the passing of the federal HIPPA laws, it is now recommended to update your powers of attorney for health care to specifically authorize your agents to review and have access to all of your medical records.

Some states have living-will acts which authorize a person to make a directive to their then-acting physician concerning the withdrawal or withholding of life-sustaining treatment in the event death is imminent with no chance for survival. These directives are useful for the end of life decisions; however, they are very narrow in scope and are not recommended to have as a person's only health care directive. Naming an agent for health care decisions under a health care power of attorney covers more health care issues and rests the burden of such decisions with family members or close friends chosen by the person making the power of attorney who would be in the best position to make decisions for the principal if needed.

Durable powers of attorney for property are an important estate planning tool, even if you have a trust in place. A durable power of attorney will aid in gaining access to a safe deposit box, handling tax matters and Social Security issues. If specific language is included in the power of attorney, it can also assist in handling asset transfers to a trust, gifting from a trust, and other specialized tasks. Although these forms are statutory forms, there are many choices in completing the forms, and they should not be completed without advice of counsel, and the powers granted should not be given without careful thought as to the availability and trustworthiness of the proposed agents.

Only Two Things in Life Are Sure—Estate Tax Laws

A person's gross estate for estate tax purpose includes the value of all assets owned by a person at the time of death, including proceeds of life insurance, annuities, IRAs, 401(k) accounts, pension and profit-sharing accounts, real estate, tangible personal, bank accounts, and investments of all kinds.

The "applicable exclusion amount" is the amount of property which will be excluded from the taxable estate for *federal* estate tax purposes. The applicable exclusion amount will be changing over the next several years, as follows:

Year	Applicable Exclusion Amount
2005	$1,500,000
2006	$2,000,000
2007	$2,000,000
2008	$2,000,000
2009	$3,500,000
2010	No Estate Tax
2011	$1,000,000

The phase-in of the current law makes planning very difficult. For younger people with modest estates, it may be difficult to decide whether trust planning is necessary. To be conservative, any single person or married couple with assets over $1,000,000 should consider trust planning for estate taxes. Most people at or beyond retirement age should seriously consider trust planning, taking into consideration lifetime disability and the possibility that trust documents may not be able to be amended if the grantor becomes permanently disabled.

After a person has designed an estate plan to fully use that person's applicable tax-exclusion amount (as well as the applicable exclusion of the spouse), further stages of estate planning should be considered. Such advanced planning is usually separated into (1) providing liquidity to pay estate taxes, (2) fully using annual exclusion amount gifting, and (3) the lifetime use of the applicable exclusion amounts.

Chapter VIII

Understanding Basic Asset Protection Principles
By Richard T. Reibman

It's Better to Plan Ahead

"911," answered the operator in the emergency command center.

"I need to talk to an insurance agent," explained the voice at the other end of the phone.

"Ma'am," the indignant staffer replied, "this is the emergency 911 center."

"I need to speak with an insurance agent," the voice insisted.

"Ma'am," the staffer continued, "this is the 911 emergency center. Calling for anything other than a life, death, or property emergency is a felony."

"That's why I need an insurance agent," the agitated woman replied. "My house is on fire, and I'm in it!"

It's been said that borrowing money from a bank is much harder to do if you actually *need* the money. Likewise, protecting assets is something that must be done before there is a need for it, because most, if not all, asset-protection plans fail if the owner of the assets waits for the crisis to occur before acting.

What sorts of crisis may occur that could devastate the portfolio you've worked so hard to build? Imagine that, leaving a party, you are involved in a traffic accident that leaves someone permanently disabled, and it is found that your alcohol content is over the legal limit.

Or perhaps you work in a field where the word "malpractice" has become commonplace, and you suddenly find yourself named as a defendant in a lawsuit claiming you did your job improperly, resulting in damages to your client or patient.

Asset protection entails how best to insulate property that you own in the event a money judgment is entered against you in a legal proceeding and the judgment creditor seeks to enforce the judgment by seizing some or all of your assets. The question becomes, is there something that could be done *today*, as a way to plan for this situation if it arises in the *future*?

With certain exceptions that are discussed below, the general rule of law is that all of your property, both real estate and personal property, is subject to the claim of a creditor holding a judgment against you. As a result, a person who has accumulated assets and a meaningful net worth would be foolhardy not to consider and implement asset-protection planning.

Because a viable asset-protection plan offers some level of protection against future claims that may or may not arise, the correct starting point for examining the type of plan that may best suit your needs begins with understanding what types of claims you might face.

Insurable Claims

Some claims arise by the nature of your business, profession, or trade. For example, if you are an accountant, physician, or attorney, you face the risk of a malpractice case resulting in a large judgment. Where insurance can cover the risk, the existence of the insurance policy, by itself, becomes a substantial portion of the asset-protection plan.

Likewise, risks posed to others by reason of your ownership of real estate, or driving a car, or serving on the board of directors of a corporation can be managed with insurance. Sometimes, all of the risk can be sheltered, while in other instances, insurance alone will not suffice as the sole asset-protection plan.

Where insurance is available to reduce or eliminate your exposure, you must carefully evaluate what sorts of risks need to be insured and how much insurance you need. Work with credible, well-established insurance experts in evaluating your needs, and whatever you do, get more than one opinion.

Unfortunately, however, there are many risks for which insurance provides no protection at all. For example, if you own a business that has borrowed money from a bank, and you have personally guaranteed repayment of the loan, there is no insurance policy that could ever protect you from the future possibility of losing your assets in order to satisfy the guaranty. Likewise, if you are a commodity futures broker executing orders for customers, there is no insurance available to protect you from losses that may arise from your errors and omissions.

Protecting Assets by Operation of Law

As explained above, understanding the potential risks that require protection is critical to putting together a viable asset-protection plan. You also need to understand the law in the state where you live. This is because all states provide for some type of "exemption" laws. Exemptions are certain assets which, by operation of law, cannot be seized by a creditor to satisfy a judgment.

For example, in Illinois, a creditor holding a judgment against a homeowner can get control of all but $7,500 in value ($15,000 if married) of a house that is being sold to satisfy a judgment. In modern times, we might agree that the "homestead exemption" (as it is commonly known) is not very valuable in Illinois. In other states, however, such as Florida and Texas, there is an *unlimited* homestead exemption. What that means, for example, is that an anesthesiologist who lives in a $5-million house in Dallas (with no mortgage) would not lose his house if he lost a major malpractice case. Is it any wonder that individuals in high-risk occupations frequently have a considerable portion of their net worth in their principal residence if they live in a state that has an unlimited homestead exemption?

Some states offer protection through operation of law by means of a method of holding title to property commonly known as "tenancy by the entirety." In some states, holding title in tenancy by the entirety is limited to real estate, while other states permit it for personal property as well. In general terms, and leaving aside the nuances in different states, tenancy by the entirety shields from creditors any property where the judgment is against only one owner, but not both. Some states require that the owners be married. Other limitations may also apply depending on where you live. For example, Illinois offers this method of holding title only to (*a*) real estate, (*b*) which is a principal residence, (*c*) owned by husband and wife. Thus, in some states, such as Illinois, simply taking title to your new home in one form of ownership as opposed to another can be a significant asset-protection tool.

Other exemptions may or may not exist in the state where you live that could affect the design of an asset-protection plan. For example, some states exempt from creditor's claims the assets in an IRA or 401k plan, while others don't. Building a large retirement account thus serves two important purposes in states where the accounts are largely or totally exempt; your account can grow tax free (until withdrawals), and creditors can't attach it; all of which is quite an incentive to make the maximum contributions possible to such plans.

In other respects, state law may dictate the shape of your asset-protection plan. For example, Wisconsin has a statute that caps the damages that can be imposed on physicians who are defendants in malpractice cases. A sound asset-protection plan for a surgeon practicing in northern Illinois may be to relocate a few miles north to southern Wisconsin in order to take advantage of laws friendlier to physicians.

On the other hand, it is usually the case that the law *protects* rather than inhibits the rights of certain types of creditors, such as divorced spouses and minor children. If your intention is to shield your assets from claims of alimony and child support, you are probably wasting your time by investing in a plan designed to avoid those claims, just as it would be foolish to believe that you could avoid payment of income taxes by implementing some sort of asset-protection plan.

In summary, basic factors such as your occupation and place of residence may dictate the basic shape of your asset-protection plan. At a minimum, these factors are the correct starting point in formulating the need for and design of your plan. The advice of an attorney or able financial planner will be instrumental in this process.

Balancing Protection with Control

All plans struggle with balancing the need for control of the asset with protection of the asset. Obviously, if an asset is not yours, your creditors cannot seize upon it. Thus, providing for the security and management of the asset, while parting with title, is not easy to do. At the same time, an asset-protection plan that imposes a material tax burden may not be justified unless your circumstances are unique.

How should title to your asset be held? Only your own attorney and advisors can provide you with advice tailored to your circumstances. However, regardless of your circumstances, certain general principles are observed.

If you are in a high-risk business or venture and your spouse is not, it might make sense to have more assets in your spouse's name. Sometimes, gifting assets to your children may be strategic for asset-protection purposes, but these decisions must be balanced against the credit-shelter exemption found in estate and gift-tax laws, which may make it more economically advantageous to keep a certain amount of assets in your own name in order to reduce the tax burden on the estate of the last to die of you and your spouse. Factors such as age, health, size of your and your spouse's estates, and whether you are actively employed in a high-risk occupation would need to be evaluated by you and your advisors in determining the correct balance.

Many clients have estate plans where the operative planning document is called a "revocable trust" or "self-directed trust." Holding title to assets in these trusts generally provides no asset protection because the grantor of the trust retains an interest in the trust, which can be attacked by creditors.

On the other hand, an "irrevocable" trust may offer asset protection because the grantor has given up any interest in the assets transferred into the trust. This, though, must be balanced against the grantor's need for control of the assets.

Holding assets in a family limited partnership may provide some degree of asset protection, because generally a creditor cannot get to the assets owned by the partnership. The creditor typically can only obtain what is called a "charging order" that enables the creditor to attach whatever it is the debtor receives from the partnership. Conceivably, if the partnership makes no distributions to the debtor, there is nothing to attach. Whether a creditor could convince a court to order distributions to be made is uncertain.

Of course, if you are self-employed and operating as a sole proprietor, you should consider whether to incorporate your business due to the well-established, limited liability benefits provided by incorporation.

Finally, many clients inquire about offshore trusts as a means of insulating assets from creditors. For the average person, an offshore trust poses certain complications and expenses that must be carefully evaluated with personal financial advisors before plunging ahead. The benefits are generally not as clear as some writers have suggested. For example, to the extent you retain any interest in an offshore account or trust, you would likely be required to disclose your interest if a creditor was attempting to enforce a judgment against you. Depending on the type of interest you hold, a judge might have the power to order you to surrender your interest, and your failure to do so could place you in contempt of court. Get the opinion of more than one reputable advisor before implementing an offshore trust as part of an asset-protection plan.

When to Plan

As stated early on, you must implement your plan before there's a need for it. This is because all states have what is commonly known as "fraudulent transfer" or "fraudulent conveyance" laws. There are different types of fraudulent transfers, but the type that bears directly on asset-protection planning is where you (the transferor) transfer assets to someone else (the transferee) in order to make it more difficult for your creditors to seize upon the property that has been transferred. An obvious example would be deeding your vacation home to your trustworthy brother (whom you know will deed it right back to you later if you ask him to) after you've been sued.

Courts generally examine several factors in determining whether property has been transferred with actual intent to hinder, delay, or defraud creditors. These factors may include whether the transfer was to a family member, whether the transfer was concealed, whether the transfer consisted of all of the transferor's assets, whether the transferor received anything in exchange for the assets transferred, and whether the transfer occurred shortly before or shortly after a substantial debt was incurred. This last factor highlights the importance of doing your planning before the problem arises.

The law does not countenance these types of transfers, and a substantial body of law has grown in this area. Sometimes, these transfers are quite obvious on their face, and judges are quick to grant relief to the creditors. Relief might mean allowing the creditor to undo the transfer or have an action against the transferee. Moreover, there is a "look back" on fraudulent transfers that can be as long as four years in some states.

So, when should you plan? There are many timely opportunities. You might plan when you are formulating your estate plan. If you have a family business that will be passed down to the next generation, you may want to plan when you are formulating your succession plan. Plan in consideration of your retirement goals. Plan in consideration of your life insurance and liability insurance needs. For example, some states exempt from creditors' reach the cash value of certain life insurance and annuity products. Understanding the laws in your state at the time you buy these products may direct how you buy them and how much you buy.

Your attorney or financial planner can help you implement a plan that addresses your personal needs and goals.

> *Her lies Lester Moore, took shots from a .44—No Les, no Moore.*
>
> —Epitaph on graveyard headstone in Tombstone, Arizona

In Conclusion

Making Intelligent Choices: The Difference Between Brokers and Advisors

You've likely noticed that Wall Street professionals—active fund managers and commissioned investment salespeople—have not exactly received glowing praise within our writings. This is because sales people receive incentive to sell and recommend specific *products*. To do so, they provide advice or utilize *your* money to achieve *their* goals. Clearly, *their* objectivity regarding *your* goals is subject to compromise.

You've also, no doubt, noticed that even though you understand the concepts of portfolio allocation, the need for planning your retirement, and the need to plan your estate, your ability to handle the details of such undertakings are limited by—not only by lack of experience, but—the professional credentials needed to affect the transactions.

Professional portfolio advisors, attorneys, and planners, on the other hand, provide *fee-based* services which help you attain your investment, retirement, and estate goals without being influenced by the need to sell a certain product—or any product at all, for that matter.

Professional advisors can provide you with an array of services and advice that cannot be obtained by lay people. It should be built upon three cornerstones:

1. Broad asset class diversification
2. Passive investment management
3. Low fund expenses

Actually, Less *Is* More

Whether you choose to work with an advisor or do it alone, you must, above all else, establish a framework that will insulate you from making emotional decisions while at the same time nurturing a long-term view for making decisions. This is the basis for a sustainable financial strategy.

In his book the *Paradox of Choice: Why More is Less,* Professor Barry Schwartz, of Swarthmore College, uses current research to demonstrate that having fewer choices in our daily lives reduces much of the stress and anxiety we experience each day. The strategies illustrated in this book are designed to simplify the financial decisions that we all face. It is our hope and prayer that this will lead to a more peaceful, content, and rewarding existence for all who implement these values and beliefs.

Self Test: Do I Need an Investment Advisor?

1. I do not plan to retire for twenty years and have a six-figure sum in cash.
2. I am a wealthy retiree on paper but don't know how I will cover my next six months' expenses.
3. I do not have a will.
4. I have a will, but it has not been reviewed by anyone for five years.
5. I have planned to "get around to" reviewing my investment selection for so long that I can't remember how long it has been.
6. The selection of holdings in my portfolio was made over time without any overall asset allocation.
7. I believe owning twenty stocks is an example of diversification.
8. I plan to retire within the next fifteen, ten, five years, and I have never had to live off an income stream that came from my investments.
9. I don't know what happens to my IRA when I die, or when my spouse dies.
10. I handle all investment decisions while my spouse has never taken any responsibility for investment decisions.

If you answered "yes" to any of the foregoing, you need an investment advisor.

About the Authors

Norbert M. Mindel, JD, CPA, PFS, CFP®

For over twenty-one years, Norbert "Norm" Mindel has been a leader in the financial services industry. He began his career by starting a law firm over twenty years ago concentrating in business planning and estate planning. This expertise gave him the opportunity to become a recognized lecturer and speaker in the Midwest.

In 1984, he and his partners formed Terra Securities Corporation a NASD-registered broker dealer. Norm played a significant role in growing the firm to over $3 billion in invested assets, with over 1,200 registered representatives. At Terra, he became a noted national speaker in several areas of expertise including asset management and estate planning. He has also been quoted on CNNfn, *Investment News*, *Chicago Tribune*, and has made several appears on CNBC's

Power Lunch. Norm can also be frequently seen addressing large groups of financial planners and accounting professionals.

Seeing the need to grow Terra aggressively, Norm developed a business and growth strategy for Terra, which eventually resulted in the sale of Terra in 1998 to GE Financial. GE Financial is part of GE, a company with unsurpassed resources and a one-hundred-year history of leadership, growth, and financial strength. GE Financial is now Genworth Financial. Terra Securities Corporation and Terra Financial Planning Group, Ltd. are now Genworth Financial Securities Corporation and Genworth Financial Advisers Corporation. At Terra, he is an executive vice president in charge of the direct management of over $1.5 billion of client assets. His other responsibilities included business development, strategic investments, acquisitions, and product development for GE Financial as well as helping representatives plan for their affluent clients.

Beginning in 2001, Norm reduced his role at Terra, so he could devote more time working with his clients.

In his role as a financial advisor, he assists individuals and business owners in meeting their financial, tax, retirement, estate planning, and ownership succession goals.

Norm is a member of the American Institute of Certified Public Accountants, Illinois State Bar Association, and the Financial Planning Association. He is also a former lecturer of accounting at the Stuart School of Business at IIT and Illinois Benedictine College. He is a licensed attorney, certified public accountant, certified financial planner and has earned the designation as a personal financial planning specialist from the American Institute of Certified Public Accountants.

Norm is a graduate of Illinois Institute of Technology ('73) and Chicago-Kent College of Law ('78). Mr. Mindel lives in Naperville, Illinois, with his wife of thirty-one years Judith and four children (Rachel, Ariel, Talia, and Zachary). His interests include history, travel, cars, and photography.

Mr. Mindel can be reached at:
Forum Financial Management, LLC
1900 S. Highland Ave., Suite 100
Lombard, Illinois 60148
Telephone: 630-873-8530
Facsimile: 630-873-8536
E-mail: nmindel@forumllc.com

Marcus K. Heinrich, CFP®

Marcus learned the importance of saving at an early age. As the son of a German immigrant bricklayer, he watched his parents work hard to secure the American dream of a better life. At the age of fourteen, Marcus began working in the construction business with his father to put himself through college. In high school, Marcus played football and was a member of his 1975 high school wrestling team, state champions that year. Marcus went on to graduate from the University of Illinois College of Engineering in 1980 as a member of the Engineering Honor Society. A few years after graduating from college, Marcus became one of the original principals of The Terra Financial Companies, Ltd., a fledgling financial services firm in Oak Brook, Illinois. He has been a certified financial planner licensee since 1988.

As an entrepreneur, Marcus was instrumental in growing Terra, a six-person financial-services firm, into a national, multidisciplinary financial-services organization with over 1,200 affiliated representatives, and over fifty employees. While there, he also helped train hundreds of financial advisors and was on the investment management committee.

Marcus became an executive vice president of Terra Securities Corporation, a GE Financial company. GE Financial is now Genworth Financial. Terra Securities Corporation and Terra Financial Planning Group, Ltd. are now Genworth Financial Securities Corporation and Genworth Financial Advisers Corporation.

In his role as a financial advisor, he assists individuals and business owners in meeting their financial, retirement, and ownership-succession goals.

Marcus is a member of the Financial Planning Association, a former board member of the Chicago Society of the Institute of Certified Financial Planners, and a former board member of the Oak Brook Association of Commerce & Industry. He was accredited by the Washington DC-based National Council on Aging to conduct their retirement planning workshop in the late 1980s. Marcus has appeared on CNN, WGN radio, and has been quoted in numerous media sources. He has spoken frequently, at both a local and national level, on retirement and investment planning.

Marcus's unique background provides a unique perspective in helping clients who are contemplating the sale of their business or preparing to retire.

Marcus lives in the far western suburbs of Chicago with his three children (Rhys, twenty; Clayton, eighteen; and Paige, fifteen). He is a loving and involved father and can often be seen, amusingly, trying to keep up with his teenagers at the gym.

Mr. Heinrich can be reached at:
Forum Financial Management, LLC.
1900 S. Highland Ave., Suite 100
Lombard, Illinois 60148
Telephone: 630-873-8510
Facsimile: 630-873-8536
E-mail: mheinrich@forumllc.com

David Strulowitz, JD, LLM

David Strulowitz's clientele consist of successful Chicago and North Shore professionals, business owners, and retirees. His clients confirm that Strulowitz, a Lincolnwood-based financial advisor, makes smart financial decisions that have helped them accumulate significant assets and enabled them to look forward to maintaining a lifestyle they desire. His knowledge, expertise, and experience make him an invaluable person in their lives.

David's prior experience includes the role of senior vice president for Terra Securities Corporation, a GE financial company, where he managed national support teams and was responsible for the financial-planning activities of over 1,200 accountants nationally. GE Financial is now Genworth Financial. Terra Securities Corporation and Terra Financial Planning Group, Ltd. are now Genworth Financial Securities Corporation and Genworth Financial Advisers Corporation. He began his career as a tax attorney who helped clients with estate and financial matters.

He earned a bachelor of science degree in business and accounting from the Boston University School of Management, and his Juris Doctorate (JD) from Boston University School of Law. He received his master of laws (LLM) in taxation from New York University School of Law. Before transitioning to financial advising, he was a tax and estate-planning attorney at Dunn Pashman Attorneys At Law, where he provided estate—and financial-planning services.

Strulowitz has both spoken and written extensively on financial, estate, and tax planning matters, including a quarterly investment newsletter and an extensive review of estate—and financial-planning software for *CPA Software News*.

A firm believer in giving back to the community, he recently completed a term as president of the board of directors of his children's school. He continues to be involved as an active member of the board and finance committees. He is a loving and involved husband and father. He and his wife, Sue, live on Chicago's North Shore with their four children: Ari, eighteen; Dana, sixteen; Molly, twelve; Jack, nine.

Mr. Strulowitz can be reached at:
Pinnacle Financial Services
Smart decisions for North Shore family wealth.
6731 N. Lincoln Avenue
Lincolnwood, Illinois 60712
Telephone: 847-679-9180
Facsimile: 847-679-9145
E-mail: dstrulow@pinfs.com

Appendix

I. Where "DALBAR" is referred to, source is

DALBAR, Inc.
Federal Reserve Plaza
600 Atlantic Avenue
Boston, MA 02210
www.dalbar.com

II. Sources and Descriptions:

Sources and Description of Asset Class Data Used in This Book Are Listed Below

U.S. Large Cap Growth

Using the DFA Large Company Portfolio, which is comprised of most of the stocks in the S&P 500. These are generally the largest market-capitalization stocks and as a group represent approximately 80 percent of the total market capitalization of all publicly traded stocks. Data Used: Jan. 1926-Dec. 1990, S&P Returns, Jan. 1991-present, DFA Large Company Portfolio.

U.S. Large Cap Value

Using the DFA Large Cap Value Portfolio, which is comprised of securities of U.S. companies, whose market capitalization falls within the largest 90 percent of the market universe. A value screen is then applied. A value stock must have a book-to-market (BtM) ratio in the upper tenth percentile. This BtM sort excludes companies with negative or zero book values. Data Used: July 1926-Mar. 1993, Fama/French U.S. Large Value (ex-utilities), simulated portfolio (lrgvalxu.sim) April 1993-present, Dimensional U.S. Large Cap Value Portfolio.

U.S. Small Cap Growth

Using the DFA Small Cap Portfolio, which is comprised of stocks whose market capitalization falls within the smallest 8 percent of the market universe. Data Used: Jan. 1973-Sept. 1988 DFA,CRSP Database

(AMEX, NYSE, & NASDAQ); Oct. 1988-Mar. 1992, CRSP Database (AMEX, NYSE, & NMS); April 1992-Mar. 2001, DFA U.S. 6-0 Small Company Portfolio, April 2001-present, DFA U.S. Small Cap Portfolio.

U.S. Small Cap Value

Using the DFA Small Cap Value Portfolio, which is comprised of stocks of U.S. companies whose market capitalization falls within the smallest 8 percent of the market universe. A value screen is then applied and a value stock typically has a high book value in relation to their market value. Data Used: July 1926-Mar. 1993, Fama/French U.S. Small Value (ex-utilities), Simulated Portfolio (smlvalxu.sim); April 1993-Mar. 2001 DFA 6-10 Value Portfolio, April 2001-present, DFA U.S. Small Value Cap Portfolio.

International Large Cap

Using the DFA Large Cap International Portfolio, which is comprised of stocks of large non-U.S. companies from "developed markets." Countries such as Australia, Denmark, France, Germany, Hong Kong, Italy, Japan, and United Kingdom are used. Data Used: Jan. 1970-Jul. 1991, MSCI EAFE Index—Net Dividends, Aug. 1991-present, DFA Large Cap International Portfolio, Countries: Japan, United Kingdom, Germany, Australia, Netherlands, Switzerland, France, and Italy.

International Large Cap Value

Using the DFA International Value Portfolio, which is comprised of stocks of large non-U.S. companies from "developed markets." Countries such as Australia, Denmark, France, Germany, Hong Kong, Italy, Japan, and United Kingdom are used. A value screen is then applied, and a value stock typically has a high book value in relation to their market value. Data Used: Jan. 1975-Mar. 1993 Intl High BtM (value) Val-Wtd Unhedged $ (Top 30% BtM) Simulated DFA Strategy (Max Japan 38%), Courtesy Fama/French + MSCI Includes Jpn, GB, Frnc, Ger, Swtz, Neth, HngKng, Aust, It, Bg Sp (Rebal Qtrly) April 1993-Jun. 1993 MSCI EAFE Index Substituted Temporarily, July 1993-Feb. 1994 DFA Intl High Book to Market Portfolio, Mar. 1994-present DFA Intl Value Portfolio.

International Small Cap Growth

Using the DFA International Small Company Portfolio, which is comprised of stocks of smaller non-U.S. companies from "developed markets." Countries such as Australia, Denmark, France, Germany, Hong

Kong, Italy, Japan, and United Kingdom are used. Data: Used Jan. 1970-Sept. 1996 Various Wts DFA Jpn, Cont, UK, Pac Rim, See Int. Dat, Oct. 1996-present DFA Intl Small Company Port.

Real-Estate Equity REITS
Using the DFA Real Estate Securities Portfolio, which is comprised of stocks from equity and hybrid real-estate investment trusts. The universe of stocks are from the NYSE, AMEX, and NASDAQ. Data Used: Jan. 1975-Dec. 1992 Simulated-Don Keim Equity REITS Index, Jan. 1993-Nov. 1994 DFA Real Estate Securities Portfolio including Residential Construction & Commercial Property Development Securities, Dec. 1994-present DFA Real Estate Securities Portfolio, REITs only.

One-Year Fixed Income
Using the DFA One-Year Fixed Income Portfolio, which is comprised mostly of high quality obligations maturing within one year from the date of settlement but can have obligations that have up to two-year maturity. Data Used: Nov. 1971-July 1983 Simulation using CD returns, Aug. 1983-present: DFA One Year Fixed Income Portfolio.

Two-Year Global Fixed Income
Using the DFA Two-Year Global Fixed Income Portfolio, which is, comprised mostly high-quality obligations, which mature within two years from the date of settlement. These obligations are issued by countries such as United States, Australia, Denmark, France, Germany, Hong Kong, Italy, Japan, and United Kingdom. Data Used: July 1952-Feb. 1996 Simulated Returns two-year maximum maturity U.S. Treasury, Data courtesy CRSP, Mar. 1996-present, DFA Two-Year Global Fixed Income Portfolio.

S&P 500
Using the S&P 500 index. Data Used: Jan. 1926-present: S&P500 Index, Source: Stocks, Bonds, Bills and Inflation, Chicago: Ibbotson and Sinquefield, 1986. Fama/French U.S. Large Value (Big High) Index Portfolio, Fama/French U.S. Large Growth (Big Low) Index Portfolio, Fama/French U.S. Small Value (Small High) Index Portfolio, Fama/French U.S. Small Growth Value (Big Low) Index Portfolio Composition: U.S. operating companies trading on the NYSE, AMEX, or NASDAQ NMS. Exclusions: ADRs, investment companies, tracking stocks, non-U.S. incorporated companies, closed-end funds, certificates, shares of beneficial interests, Berkshire Hathaway Inc. (Permco 540), and negative book

values. Source: CRSP databases for returns and market capitalizations: 1926-present. Compustat and hand-collected book values: 1926-1992. CRSP links to Compustat and hand-collected links: 1926-present. Book-to-market ratios provided by Dimensional: 1993-present. Breakpoint: The size breakpoint is the market capitalization of the median NYSE firm, so the big and small categories contain the same amount of eligible NYSE firms. The BtM breakpoints split the eligible NYSE firms positive book equity (BE) into three categories: 30% of eligible NYSE firms with positive BE are in low (Growth), 40% are in medium (Neutral), 30% are in high (Value). Rebalancing: Annual: (at end of June): 1926-1992, Quarterly: 1993-present.

CRSP, Deciles 6-10 Index
Source: CRSP, total return in USD$. Small Company Universe Returns (Deciles 6-10), All Exchanges; Oct. 1988-present: CRSP Index (NYSE, AMEX, & OTC); Jan. 1973-Sept. 1988: CRSP Databases; (NYSE & AMEX & OTC) July 1962-Dec. 1972: CRSP Databases (NYSE & AMEX), Rebalanced: Quarterly; Jan. 1926-June 1962, NYSE, Rebalanced Semi-Annually.

MSCI EAFE Index ($) Gross Div
Source: MSCI, total returns gross dividends in USD$; Jan. 1969-present: MSCI EAFE Index ($) Gross Div.

Emerging Markets Value
Using DFA Emerging Markets Value Portfolio. Total Returns net of all fees in USD$. Countries: Argentina, Brazil, Indonesia, Chile, Malaysia, Mexico, Philippines, Portugal, Thailand, Turkey, Israel, Korea, Greece. Weighted equally, rebalanced monthly. April 1998-present, DFA Emerging Markets Value Portfolio, March 1993-March 1998, Emerging Markets Closed-End Portfolio, January 1987-February 1993, Courtesy of Fama/French (*Value Vs. Growth: The International Evidence*. Journal of Finance '53 (1998), 1975-1999).

Emerging Markets Index
Using DFA Equally Weighted Emerging Markets Index. Countries: Argentina, Brazil, Chile, Mexico, Hungary, Poland, Czech Republic, Israel, Turkey, South Africa, Taiwan, Korea, Indonesia, Philippines, Thailand, and Malaysia. Korea was added in May 1997 as the twelfth country. Hungary and Poland were added in June 2000; Taiwan was added in June 2002. Rebalanced Monthly.

Emerging Markets Growth

Using DFA Emerging Markets Portfolio. Total returns net of all fees in USD$. Countries: Argentina, Brazil, Indonesia, Chile, Malaysia, Mexico, Philippines, Portugal, Thailand, Turkey, Israel, Korea, Greece. Weighted equally, rebalanced monthly. May1994-present, DFA Emerging Markets Portfolio, March 1993-April 1994, DFA Emerging Markets Closed-End Portfolio, January 1987-February 1993, Courtesy of Fama/French (*Value Vs. Growth: The International Evidence*. Journal of Finance '53 (1998), 1975-1999).

One-Month U.S. Treasury Bills

Source: Total return net of fees in USD$. January 1926-present: one-month Treasury bills. *Stocks, Bond, Bills and Inflation*; Chicago: Ibbotson and Sinquefield, 1986.

Six-Month U.S. Treasury Bills Index

Source: January 1978-present: Merrill Lynch GO02 Index, total returns in USD$, January 1964-January 1978: CRSP.

Merrill Lynch One-Year U.S. Treasury Note Index

Source: Merrill Lynch GC03 Index, total returns in USD$.
Jul. 2000-present: ML One-Year U.S. Treasury Note Index
Jun. 1991-Jun. 2000: ML One-Year Treasury Bill Index
Jul. 1963-May 1991: CRSP/DFA.

Five-Year U.S. Treasury Notes

Source: Total return net of fees in USD$. January 1926-present, five-year treasury notes. Source: Ibbotson Intermediate Five-Year Treasury Notes.

Long Term Government Bonds

Source: Total return net of fees in USD$. January 1926-present, long-term government bonds. *Stocks, Bond, Bills and Inflation*; Chicago: Ibbotson and Sinquefield, 1986.